ENDURING
PATAGONIA

RANDOM HOUSE NEW YORK

GREGORY CROUCH

ENDURING

PATAGONIA

All rights reserved under International and Pan-American Copyright Conventions.
Published in the United States by Random House, Inc., New York, and simultaneously
in Canada by Random House of Canada Limited, Toronto.

RANDOM HOUSE and colophon are registered trademarks of Random House, Inc.

A portion of this book was originally published in the March 2000 issue of National Geographic.

Library of Congress Cataloging-in-Publication Data
Crouch, Gregory.
Enduring Patagonia / Gregory Crouch.
p.   cm.
ISBN 0-375-50434-6 (alk. paper)
1. Patagonia (Argentina and Chile)—Description and travel. 2. Andes—Description and travel.
3. Mountaineering—Patagonia (Argentina and Chile) 4. Snow and ice climbing—Patagonia
(Argentina and Chile) 5. Crouch, Gregory—Journeys—Patagonia (Argentina and Chile) I. Title.
F2851 .C78   2001
918.2'70464—dc21   2001019416

Random House website address: www.atrandom.com

Printed in the United States of America on acid-free paper

9 8 7 6 5 4 3 2

First Edition

Illustrations on pages 215, 216, 217, and 221 by Jackie Aher
Book design by Barbara M. Bachman

To my wife, DeAnne, my best friend and biggest support,
and
to those with whom I have shared the rope in Patagonia:

Jim Donini, Alex Hall, Stefan Hiermaier, Charlie Fowler,
Thomas Ulrich, David Fasel, Stefan Siegrist, Boris Strmšek,
J. Jay Brooks, Pablo Besser, Waldo Farias, Robyn Bunch,
Steve Schraeder, and Andrés Zegers.

This would not have been possible without you.

Chief among these motives was the overwhelming idea of the great whale himself. Such a portentous and mysterious monster roused all my curiosity. Then the wild and distant seas where he rolled his island bulk; the undeliverable, nameless perils of the whale; these, with all the attending marvels of a thousand Patagonian sights and sounds, helped to sway me to my wish. With other men, perhaps, such things would not have been inducements; but as for me, I am tormented with an everlasting itch for things remote. I love to sail forbidden seas, and land on barbarous coasts.

HERMAN MELVILLE, *Moby-Dick.*

ACKNOWLEDGMENTS

THANKS TO ALL THE EDITORS WHO HAVE worked with me and my Patagonian writings: especially DeAnne Musolf Crouch, who has been there through all of it; Lee Boudreaux at Random House (this project has been lucky from the get-go); Steve Roper, Allen Steck, and Ed Webster at *Ascent;* Joan Tapper at *Islands;* Oliver Payne at *National Geographic;* Alison Osius and Jeff Achey at *Climbing;* and George Bracksieck and Dougald MacDonald at *Rock & Ice;* and to Robert Legault for his diligent copyediting.

To Ronald Goldfarb, my dream agent, who does exactly what he says he's going to do when he says he's going to do it, and the first person besides DeAnne to share my vision for *Enduring Patagonia.*

All those with whom I've climbed in Patagonia deserve special thanks. We kept one another safe, did some radical stuff, and made it down from some of the world's most wild places.

To Rolando Garibotti, for friendship and inspiration—no man on earth knows more about the mountains of Patagonia.

To Thomas Ulrich, Charlie Fowler, and Jim Donini, for access to their photo collections.

To my many friends in Chaltén: Susana Queiro, the soul of Argentina's Parque Nacional de los Glaciares, and her husband, Ricardo Sanchez; Roxana Arbilla of Piedra del Fraile (a good chunk of my first draft was written there); Javier Maceira, Rodrigo Mazzola, Gabriel Fassio, Mariana Hardoy, Patricia Barría, and Sandra Maigua of Rancho Grande (where I wrote the other great chunk of my first draft); Anabel Machiñena and Mariana Villanueva of La Chocolatería; Marcelo Pagani and Doctora Carolina Codó of El Pilar; Andrea Neelsen, Pablo Cottescu, and Ana Queija of La Ruca Mahuida; Mirta Levi and Raúl Cardozo of La Casita; Rubén Vázquez and Ester Havermanns of the Albergue Patagonia; Ivó Domenec of La Senyera and Estancia Canigó; Miguel Burgos of La Boticueva; Don Rodolfo Guerra and his wife, Isolina Ogrizek; Max O'Dell; Marcela Antonutti; Gerardo Javier Spisso; Hernan Salas; Alberto del Castillo; Horacio Codó; and María Ines Leyenda of Estancia Maipú.

To Kevin Trenberth of the National Center for Atmospheric Research for helping me understand the weather processes of the Southern Hemisphere. Any mistakes included herein are mine and mine alone.

So many others deserve thanks: Franci Novak, Thomas Kocar, Silvana Albano, Adriana Albano, Luis Roberto Albano, Lojze Kocur, Jani Kocmur, Stanko Hrovat, Janko Vidmar, Soames Floweree, Silvo Karo, José Luis Fonrouge, John Bragg, Jon Krakauer, Tom Strickler, Brian Lipson, Jenny Mathew, Viju Mathew, and Mr. Mathew, Kent McClannan, Bruce Miller, Doug Byerly, Jimmy Surette, Forrest Murphy, Yvon Chouinard, Miyazaki Motohiko, Athol Whimp, Andrew Lindblade, John Fantini, Simon Parsons, the Zegers family of Santiago, Ross Johnson, Michele Hanson, Greg Corliss, Phil Krichilsky, Mary Beth Krichilsky, Frank Macon, Brian Coppersmith, Nelly Avila, Marta Conforti, Dani and Mari and Emmanuel Alonso, Joseph Conrad, Antoine de Saint-Exupéry, and Beryl Markham.

CONTENTS

ENDURING

PATAGONIA

An OTHERWORLDLY RANGE OF MOUNTAINS exists in Patagonia, at the southern end of the Americas. It is a sublime range, where ice and granite soar with a dancer's grace. From the mountains' feet tumble glaciers and dark forests of beech. The summits float in the southern sky, impossibly remote. Climbers who gaze upon these wonders ache to unlock their secrets. Hard, steep, massive, these might be our planet's most perfect mountains.

To court these summits is to graft fear to your heart, for all is not idyllic beauty among the great peaks of Patagonia. They stand squarely athwart what sailors refer to as the "roaring forties" and "furious fifties"—that region of the Southern Hemisphere between 40° and 60° south latitude known for ferocious wind and storm. The violent weather spawned over the great south sea charges through the Patagonian Andes with gale-force wind, roaring cloud, and stinging snow. Buried like a rapier deep into the heart of the southern ocean, Patagonia is a land trapped between angry torrents of sea and sky.

The horrendous weather more than makes up for the fact

that the mountains of Patagonia do not count extreme altitude as a weapon. Altitude is only one aspect of climbing difficulty. The enormous walls of Patagonia demand fast, efficient, and expert practice of every climbing technique. Wealthy dilettantes cannot buy their way onto these exclusive summits. Only years of dedication to the alpine trade earn a climber the right to gain a Patagonian summit.

Cerro Fitzroy and Cerro Torre are the two crown jewels of the range. Seen from across the wind-swept scrub of the steppes to the east, they are the two crux battlements in the long Andean rampart. Far outdoing the Great Pyramids, Fitzroy's stone bulk towers 10,000 feet over the arid plains and dominates the landscape like a barbarian king. Beside and a bit behind the king rises Cerro Torre, his royal consort, a graceful obelisk: tall, slender, vertiginous, elusive, hers the very form of alpine perfection. Although Fitzroy is a few hundred feet taller, Cerro Torre exceeds the king in every aspect except size—in difficulty, in threat, in promise, in beauty, in subtlety, and in the savageness of her fury. Cerro Fitzroy and Cerro Torre shoulder the sky like titans.

Cerro Torre stands at the left end of a line of towers, all divided from Fitzroy and his satellites by a deep valley and a flowing glacier. Fitzroy's half-dozen satellites form a horseshoe to the left and right of the king. Anywhere else, the peaks that flank Fitzroy and Cerro Torre would be centerpiece summits; here in Patagonia they are the palace guard.

Beyond the mountains to the west lies the Southern Patagonian Ice Cap. The ice cap runs north-south like a long irregular cigar, bounded on one side by the front range of the Andes, and on the other by the Pacific Ocean. At its widest point, twenty-five miles north of the Fitzroy massif, the ice cap is almost sixty miles across. At its narrowest, sixty miles south of Fitzroy, less than ten miles of ice separate the Pacific Ocean in Fiordo Peel from fresh waters that flow into the Brazo

Mayor (the major arm) of Lago Argentino. From north to south the ice cap is 225 miles long, and without counting the many glaciers that drain it, the surface of the ice cap measures more than 5,000 square miles. It is our world's largest nonpolar expanse of ice and one of the least knowable landscapes on earth. From no point in the settled world can one get a true impression of the ice cap, for the Andes block the view of it from the inhabited desert to the east. There are places from which we can observe the glaciers that drain the ice cap through breaks in the mountain chain, and from other points we can view bits and pieces of the ice fields, but the ice cap itself exists almost in myth, in a world beyond men. No man makes his home there, and only the most intrepid access this frozen fastness—and even they cannot stay for long.

Driven ashore by the remorseless west wind, storms blast out of the southern ocean, seethe over the ice cap, and guard the summits of the Patagonian Andes with Olympian fury. The leading edge of a storm often reveals Fitzroy as a threatening shadow within the churning clouds, but of Cerro Torre there is seldom any trace. Typically, the storm expends its moisture on the ice cap and mountains, but the power of the wind remains as it bursts free of the peaks and surges across the steppes east of the Andes. Above the desert steppes the west wind strings the clouds out into stacks and lines of saucer- and cigar-shaped lenticular clouds, clouds that run downwind and fade into the blue sky until all that remains of the storms is the wind, the gusting wind, the ceaseless, ceaseless wind.

When rare clear skies greet the rising sun, Fitzroy, Cerro Torre, and their satellites are bathed with purple, blue, rose, and gold light. In such outlandish beauty, the ice and stone heights seem to hold forth the ultimate promise. But late in the day, when the sun sinks to the west, those same mountain faces are shadowed and ominous, iron-bound like the walls of Dante's City of Dis. Then, as the sun drops unseen into the ice cap beyond the mountains, hellfire burns atop the mountain rampart.

Stories of fear, suffering, and failure stop most climbers from coming to Patagonia, and the stories accurately reflect reality. The mountains have no generosity and no justice. They stand unmoved by the human dramas that play out on their flanks, and they give and take with unknowable whim. We have only the dignity of persistence with which to combat this terrible faceless indifference.

The Patagonian gauntlet of hardship cannot be evaded. Frustration builds for climbers as attempt after arduous attempt is rejected by southern storms. Few have the mental fortitude to withstand the repeated failures coupled with the extended inactivity the bad weather enforces. But there are a handful of climbers who find the opposing miseries of the Patagonian Andes irresistible and are repeatedly drawn to this proving ground.

For many years I have been just such a human comet, in long orbits around the obelisks of Patagonia. Seven times I've made the pilgrimage. And I will go back, for the times that I spend in those mountains are the most charged moments of my life. In the mountains, life sings. Normal life can be such drudgery; little seems important. But in the mountains, all is different, for the alpine life is a life of consequence. In Patagonia every act, every choice, is significant. The myriad moods of the world matter. Has the wind shifted? Did the clouds rise or lower? Has it snowed much recently? Did it freeze last night? Climbers in the Patagonian Andes are as subject to the tyrannies of wind and storm as were the sailors in the age of tall wooden ships. The pulse of the world ran through their veins, and, in the mountains, it runs through mine.

I first arrived in Patagonia, the better part of a decade ago, with a torn backpack, battered tennis shoes, a few hundred dollars in my pocket, my ragged passport, and two letters from my girlfriend about the shaky ground we stood on. Nagging somewhere behind were the never-ending expectations of my driven, success-oriented mother and father for their West Point graduate but otherwise disappointing son. I had followed a dream to the peaks of Patagonia, but, nearing thirty, I was too old for purposeless endeavor, too uninterested in the cubicle world of the corporate workplace to build a career, and far too much in love with mountains to abandon them.

Now, my Patagonian adventures shimmer in my memory with the hammered silver look of the sun on wind-ruffled water. I could sort them into chronological order, but that's not how I live them. To me, these memories are a tapestry without end or beginning. On these mountain expeditions I have discovered my compass, and it is the harsh discipline of the alpine way. The same final destination awaits us all, climbers and flatlanders alike. In the meantime, there is only the path. For me, it is enough.

My Patagonia is never far buried. Whenever I pull Patagonia into the forefront of my mind, which I do many times a day, I see a vision of the great peaks as they soar up into a sky full of angry clouds. I hear the terrible wind. And I feel fear.

But why climb? And why climb in Patagonia, where storm and mountain are so cruel? I am regularly asked why and I hate the question because the answer refuses distillation, and my inability to produce an adequate quip makes me seem an inarticulate fool. There is no sentence, no paragraph that captures the answer. Virtually everything that I know I have learned in the mountains, for only in such an elemental realm is truth undiluted. Mountains, and mostly the mountains of Patagonia, have taught me what I know about terror and joy; friendship; mirth and gravity; courage and cowardice and when to take a risk; success and failure; persistence, patience, endurance, and opportunity. To them I owe my most extreme visions of beauty and most of what I know about myself. But climbing is so much more than a series of schoolmaster's lessons, and I resort to writing in the hope that when our shared journey is over you will feel the answer to the question why in your heart and guts as I feel it in mine. And if I fail at that task—as I almost certainly will—then I hope that you will at least enjoy these stories from my alpine life.

•

In Patagonia a storm clears and the alpine monoliths stand like teeth set in a dragon's jaw. The last shreds of cloud fade into the firmament. The message broadcast from the peaks is as jarring as the scream of a train whistle. "Show yourself," they say. Few moments bristle with as much opportunity. And before such uncaring majesty I wrestle my twin demons of fear and desire. Do I want this? Who am I? Is it enough? I wonder every time. Those who don't seek out such moments of beauty, passion, and intensity don't know themselves as well as they should. People may say that alpinism is a fool's game full of meaningless risk, and they may be right, but I climb because I thirst to throw back the margins of my world. There remains so much that I do not know.

CERRO TORRE IS MAKING US SUFFER AGAIN. Water drains from the snow-covered ledge above and pours down the crack where I jam my hands. The frigid water- fall soaks my gloves and storm gear. A riot of wind bellows and races through the clouds and rain. The pounding wind drives sheets of almost freezing rain at Alex Hall and me. Mas- sive updrafts blow rain at us from below. The few pregnant pauses are pure psychic agony. Chill water runs down my arms, back, buttocks, legs, and fills my leather boots. My lips are blue.

Alex belays me from below with one end of our rappel ropes. The other end is stuck over our heads—for the fourth time. These sodden ropes are unmanageable. The wild wind launches them into space the instant we pull each rappel, and our eight-millimeter descent rope wraps around every imag- inable rock protrusion. I curse myself for thinking a light rap- pel line would be useful in Patagonia. The wind owns this flimsy cord.

Alex and I have been fighting our way down from our high

point halfway up Cerro Torre's southeast ridge, the infamous Compressor Route, for the last ten hours, and here I am, battered by the elements and risking another long fall to free the damned rope again. I yank it out from behind a flake of rock, section by section. Twenty feet below, Alex traps each new length under his boot in a wet crack to make sure it won't blow loose and tangle elsewhere. Finally, I jerk the end of the thin rope loose and toss it down to Alex. He packs it into the crack and returns his attention to my belay. I climb down to join him.

"Only two more raps!" yells Alex as he rigs the ropes to a nest of rusty pitons.

"What was I thinking, bringing this fucking dental floss to Patagonia? It's useless!"

I double the two ropes and bite a V into them to help them thread through the holes in my aluminum belay/rappel plate. With the ropes pushed through the two little holes, I clip the point of the V to the locking carabiner at my waist and begin to lower myself away from the anchor. The soggy ropes make a crotch-fountain spout from my belay plate as I descend, a fountain that soaks my midsection.

I go down first on the last rappel to the glacier, and I topple down a cone-shaped slope of snow below the bergschrund and take myself off rappel. It's still raining, I'm still shivering, and the wind still screams and howls, but all we have to do is rope up and stagger down the glacier to our sleeping bags packed in plastic sacks at the Norwegian bivy, a cluster of pseudocaves and leaky rock walls in a moraine that serves as our gear stash.

We wade through a knee-deep swamp of off-white snow and eventually reach the bivy. It's nine P.M. when we crawl through a gap in the rock walls beneath a shelter stone. The roof leaks. The floor is gritty, wet, and nowhere level, but at least in the dank cave we're out of the wind and the driving rain. Alex stuffs his sleeping bag into a bivy sack, which is like a giant uninsulated potato sack designed to be water-proof, peels off his soggy storm shells and boots, crams himself into his bag, and begins to brew a long-coveted hot drink.

I sit stunned, unable to summon the energy to remove my boots. Too exhausted to move, I stare at Alex as he fumbles with the stove. My swollen hands and feet ache, and I have had no food or drink in six-teen hours. For thirty days we've been trying to climb the mountain above us. This latest rejection has set a new personal record for alpine misery—for cold, wetness, thirst, hunger, exhaustion, and pain.

"Ha," I croak. And smile.

Alex looks up from his labor. "What's so funny? We just got our asses kicked—for the sixth time."

"This is bliss, bud. This is exactly what I wanted—big Patagonian action." It isn't as bad as what I did to earn this trip. "I'd take a thou-sand beatings rather than go back in that hole in the ground working heavy construction or installing a machine in another McDonald's."

I started socking away money for this trip by working on a crew building a sewer lift station for the city of Loveland, Colorado. After the heavy construction job I took the installation gig, where I fiddled with tricky plastic parts in awkward corners littered with crushed french fries. I got hounded by hostile assistant managers who hadn't graduated from high school. I struggled to get the contraption work-ing during all-night setups, then drove like a demon to the next job site in Texas, North Dakota, or wherever. Visions of Patagonia's perfect peaks sustained me through the grimmest hours. A Denver traffic jam could become a full-fledged Patagonian storm if I freed my imagina-tion for a minute. Down south there would be no pneumatic tools, no bosses, no long drives, and no assistant managers. In Patagonia, the wind would tear away the dirt of a tough year.

Alex Hall said yes in a heartbeat when I asked him to join me for the Cerro Torre campaign. He's the guy you want reaching for you when you're neck deep in quicksand. Alex is strong and stout, even-tempered, and a good, competent, well-rounded climber—the perfect partner for a few months in the Patagonian crucible.

The morning after our sixth attempt, an atrocious wind pummels Alex and me back to base camp, Campo De Agostini, beneath the beech trees along the banks of the Río Fitzroy. Clouds of churning vanilla milkshake cover the range. Long underwear, fleece clothing, socks, hardware, and ropes adorn the trees of base camp—relics of other parties' recent epics. Of Cerro Torre there is no evidence besides our aching hands and feet. Alex and I ravenously descend on a tub of jelly, stuff slathered crackers into our mouths, and savor hot coffee.

Base camp in Patagonia is the best place I've ever called home. I love every second of stormbound base-camp time. No bills to pay, no telephones to answer, no messages to return, no errands to run, no deadlines to meet—just hedonistic rounds of coffee, chow, card games, letters, journals, novels, sleep, whiskey, wine, and conversations with climbers and trekkers from all corners of the globe. It's an uncomplicated existence, and if it weren't for the power of the peaks that lurk in the clouds, base camp would be the most peaceful place I know.

But the lure of the peaks is inescapable. Ten miles up the glacier, the spires stand sentinel over the valley's head. Cerro Torre, Torre Egger, Cerro Standhardt, Aguja (the Spanish word for "needle") Bífida, Aguja de los Cuatro Dedos, and Domo Blanco on the left; Piergiorgio and Cerro Pollone across the head of the valley; and Fitzroy, Aguja Poincenot, Torre Innominata, Aguja Saint-Exupéry, de la "S," and Mojón Rojo on the right hand. Once caught by the long shadows of the mountains, we cannot relax—and I cannot escape the fear. I feel like a soldier waiting for D-Day.

•

In the late 1950s, Cerro Torre stood unclimbed, and while most of the world's mountaineering energies were spent in the high peaks of Asia, Cerro Torre captured the imagination of some top Italian climbers. In 1958, rival factions raced to make the first ascent. Walter Bonatti and Carlo Mauri led an expedition out onto the ice cap to attempt Cerro Torre's unknown West Face while another expedition explored the Torre's more easily accessible east side.

Bonatti and Mauri reached a platform over halfway up the peak, beneath a wicked mushroom of rime ice they named the Helmet, but were unable to get past it. They left a cache of gear and hoped to return some subsequent year. As they descended through the southwest col, the high pass that separates Cerro Torre from Cerro Adela, they christened it the Col of Hope.

Meanwhile, on the opposite side of the mountain, expedition leader Bruno Detassis lost heart and declared Cerro Torre "impossible" soon after the peak emerged from a storm to show her perfect form. But two of that expedition's members, Cesare Maestri and Cesarino Fava, were not so easily deterred. Maestri and Fava, along with Austrian Toni Egger, returned the following season determined to win the Torre's magic summit, and in a desperate, all-out six-day push, Maestri and Egger, supported by Fava, claimed to have done it, starting up the East Face and finishing on the North Face. The stormy descent cost Egger his life—he was swept away by falling ice.

In a clear jab at Bonatti and Mauri, Maestri named the north col, through which he and Egger had supposedly climbed, the Col of Conquest, and wrote that "in the mountains there is no such thing as hope, only the will to conquer. Hope is the weapon of the poor."

The still virgin tower to the right of Cerro Torre was given Egger's name. Contemporaries trumpeted the Maestri-Egger climb as the greatest climb ever done, and it would certainly stand among the best ascents of the twentieth century if such a storm of controversy hadn't sprung up in the years since 1959. Not one shred of physical evidence has ever surfaced to support Maestri's claim to Cerro Torre's summit, and the camera was with Egger when he was lost. Year after year top alpinists attempt to duplicate Maestri's feat—and in forty years no one has succeeded. Indeed, those who have come closest report significant differences between the terrain they encountered and what Maestri reported.

Over a decade later, Maestri, who was still in good form past the age of forty, returned to Patagonia intending to silence his growing corps of critics by forging *another* route up Cerro Torre. This time Maestri and his team climbed the mountain's Southeast Buttress, which soars 4,500 feet and resembles the flying buttress of a Gothic cathedral. But rather than a tour de force of courage, commitment, and skill, like the purported 1959 climb, Maestri's 1970 team raised a 150-pound gas-operated air compressor up the peak with a come-along (a hand-operated winch commonly used to pull stuck vehicles out of the mud). The team strung up thousands of feet of rope to link themselves to safety, and Maestri used the compressor to drill 350 bolts up steep sections of mostly crackless stone. Climbers nicknamed Maestri's new climb the Compressor Route, and his preposterous reduction of difficulty with pneumatic construction techniques drew another storm of protest, most famously in an article called "Cerro Torre: A Mountain Desecrated," published in England in *Mountain* magazine. In fairness to Maestri, the majority of the Compressor Route does consist of hard, high-quality climbing on natural features, but Maestri's new route only added fresh venom to the old controversy.

Bonatti and Mauri's vision of a route up the West Face was finally realized in 1974, when it was scaled by an Italian team led by Casimiro Ferrari. The West Face climb stands in stark contrast to the Compressor Route. Whereas any ascent of the Compressor Route involves an embrace of Maestri's engineering because his bolt ladders are still in place, the remote, distant, more unknown West Face, which rises out of the Southern Patagonian Ice Cap, is as savage a mountain experience as a climber can hope for.

For me, the ice cap and its dangers and hardships—known and unknown—loomed too large. I lacked the courage to face the ice cap, and Torre's West Face seemed too wild, too remote, too isolated—too much. I opted to try the Compressor Route instead, and, compromised as it is, the Compressor Route is far from trivial.

•

I slap the alarm into silence. We haven't left base camp in a week. Few sounds in Patagonia are as comforting as the sound of the wild west wind as it screams through the beech trees over base camp at two o'clock in the morning. There is no point in even turning on a headlamp to check the barometer. Wind in Patagonia is a bad sign—depending on your perspective. Good weather brings fear. I am happy we won't climb tomorrow. I won't have to prove I'm not a coward; I won't have to test my drive; I won't have to back all my talk with vertical action; I won't have to find out whether or not I'm good enough to climb Cerro Torre. I snuggle deep into my warm sleeping bag, lulled back to sleep by the insane crash and rush overhead, certain that tomorrow I'll enjoy another relaxing, social, and gluttonous day in camp.

While I'm warm and alone in the night, the dark specter of my fear is also at rest. It's not idle fear: I know the terror of being caught by a storm high on the sides of one of these peaks. Even on flat ground I've been blown off my feet and thrown five yards by the wind. I'm relieved that tomorrow Alex and I won't have to toil beneath a rare cobalt-blue vault of sky, rushing to climb malevolent and magnificent Cerro Torre. The worst windows of good weather are the "almost long enough" ones—the ones that get us fully committed to the mountain, far up its flanks, and then violently shut down all progress. Then the voice of the wind, so comforting in base camp, becomes the incessant howl of the marching legions of hell. . . . Up high the wind turns the world to chaos, but here, safe in my tent, I peacefully drift back to sleep.

Eight hours later, my case of narcolepsy is temporarily cured. Finally alert, I dress and stumble through the wind and rain from my tent to the crude log hut. Four live trees frame this ramshackle hut, the combined construction effort of several seasons' worth of Patagonian hopefuls. Stacks of logs and stones hold tarpaulins and ground cloths in place and wage a constant war against the wind. Three rough-hewn log benches form a horseshoe around a stone table and a fireplace constructed of hand-stacked stones. A stovepipe made of flattened tin cans held together by nails and strategic tin-folding does a barely adequate job of clearing the smoke from the hut.

"Good morning, you scum-sucking pus-bag," I ritually insult Alex as I toss open the hut's jury-rigged door. "Goddamn, are you writing another letter?"

"Greg," replies Alex with a soothing voice and a smile, "would you like a cup of coffee?" I satisfy my first hedonistic impulse of the day and fill my coffee cup. Alex pauses between sentences of the zillionth letter to his girlfriend back in the States and points out the jam and crackers. I eat, adding to the "open-bivy surplus" growing around my midsection. Alex and I are the senior residents of Campo De Agostini. We've been here since before Thanksgiving, and now it's almost Christmas.

Jim Donini and his partner, Stefan Hiermaier of Germany, wander into the hut for coffee. That Jim has outlived his climbing résumé is as amazing as the fact that at fifty-two years old he goes after these horrendous peaks with the vitality and commitment of those of us twenty years his junior. Jim is tall, fit, lean, tough, with piercing blue eyes, a full head of gray hair, and a wide smile that crinkles his whole face. Stefan fell in with Donini climbing small crags in Utah and got talked out of a winter of warm rock climbing in the deserts of the American Southwest and into a season of action in Patagonia by Jim's tales of beautiful Patagonian granite. Donini is one hell of a salesman, because Stefan had never climbed a big alpine peak before arriving here, but he's doing well at Cerro Torre's hard school.

For lack of anything better to do, I begin my daily ball-busting. Jim, Stefan, Alex—Alex, Jim, Stefan—I run through all possible variations and worn-out themes. Donini's age, Alex's lovesickness, Stefan's nationality, Donini's divorces, Alex's good nature, and so on. Charlie Fowler pops into the hut and gives us some lip. "You be careful, Charlie," I warn him. "You'd be catching the old-man comments if it wasn't for Jim."

Stefan Siegrist, a hot young Swiss climber, packs into the crowded hut. He doesn't speak enough English to understand the ribbing directed at him. His partner, Thomas Ulrich, does, and fires back, "Greg, you would be thrown out of Switzerland for such horrible behavior." A feeding frenzy goes into full effect. Food from a plethora of containers and jars gets shoveled into half a dozen mouths. Insults fly in all directions. Coffee water heats on two gas stoves and over the fire. Peals of laughter reverberate through the hut. Swear words in several languages vault back and forth above the conversations.

Jim holds court around the low stone table from his seat beside the fire. Our heads lean forward as we revel in the gossip he has accumulated in three decades of worldwide alpine adventure. Tension builds as his story nears conclusion. Our bodies jerk upright and our heads toss back with the punch line—and so flies the dirt on yet another famous climber.

Eventually, Jim goes off for an afternoon nap. Alex and I begin a game of rummy. Nicks and stains make every face card recognizable, but the game is desperately competitive. I lurch out of the hut to relieve myself, squint through sheets of rain, and spy some restless hopeful strapped to an elaborate set of elastic cords. He does pull-ups from the trees on the other side of camp. I shake my head and return to the card game. In five weeks, I have not done a pull-up, a training session, a power hike, or a trail run. Eight years in the Army trained me to kill time with the very best.

"Sit down, scumbag," Alex says to me as I come through the door. "Your ass is mine."

"Ha! Split me off a chunk of that cheese, chump."

Alex deals another hand of cards. Jim, bleary-eyed from his nap, bumbles back into the hut, mumbling something about a rise in the pressure.

"Jesus, Jim, can you go fifteen minutes without checking the pressure?"

"I don't know, Greg, this could be the start of a big high-pressure system."

Whoop, flap, BANG!!! A tremendous gust shivers the plastic walls of the hut. "Yeah, right . . ."

"It looks like the weather might be clearing."

"Hey, Alex, pass me a box of *petróleo*. Jim here's hallucinating. . . . Anyway, it's cocktail hour." *Petróleo humano* (human fuel) is the Argentine nickname for the one-liter boxes of cheap wine that the local gauchos imbibe in monstrous quantities. I cut a corner off a box with a pocketknife and spill dirty red wine into three cups.

"Cheers, boys, here's to good weather." The tin cups chink. Cerro Torre dominates my thoughts—never in my life has anything scared me so much. I close my eyes and savor the sensation as the simple wine pours into my belly. Those twin demons of fear and desire writhe within.

Card game concluded, Alex, Jim, Charlie, Stefan, and I enjoy a lit-
erary session. One of the blessings of Patagonian climbing is catching
up on a year's worth of neglected reading. Around the fire we read *The
Idiot, For Whom the Bell Tolls, Typhoon,* Kissinger's *Diplomacy,* and Barbara
Tuchman's *A Distant Mirror,* a book on the history of the fourteenth
century. We consumed the season's quota of potboilers long ago.

I take a walk and poke my head into the other base-camp hut. A
morose French team practically sobs into their porridge bowls, and
dejected climbers slump onto benches all around. An Argentine
climber blackens her etching of the Fitzroy skyline with a heated nail.
A perfect telephone carved out of wood is mounted into one of the
hut's vertical supports. Three rotating wheels displaying the day of
the week, the date, and the month are mounted near the phone—I
have no idea if they're correct. Some joker drew a monkey seated in a
clearing in front of three abstracted Torres, the drawn Torres even
more dizzyingly terrifying than the originals. Another made a picture
frame and mounted three photos of megabeautiful Argentine model
Valeria Mazza; polished shelves and crude benches abound. Etched
flowers, stick figures, and a superb Impressionist painting of the Torres
round out the collection of time-killing creations.

Back in our hut, I try my hand at visualization while the others
continue to read. I try to imagine myself standing atop Cerro Torre
with Alex after climbing to the summit beneath calm blue skies. All I
end up with is an image of Alex and me pasted in rime ice, struggling
against wind and cloud to escape the clutches of the terrible mountain. Here, in the extreme south, I am afraid.

Alex steps out of the hut and in a moment comes rushing back inside. "Greg, Greg, she's coming out of the cloud!"

"Liar, sit back down."

"No, she really is."

The door rattles shut behind the departing crowd as they follow

Alex into the clearing in front of the hut to examine the potential break in the weather. Alone in the hut, I toss my mangled book down on the stone table, expel air from my lungs, and pick up my cup of *petróleo*. An iron hand clutches down around the joint between my esophagus and stomach. I draw cold air into my chest and raise the cup with my eyes closed; I don't want to see the wine tremble.

The few fingers of wine go down warm, earthy, and sweet, but do little to control the cold settling into my abdomen. A clank sounds loud and harsh when I toss the empty cup into the dirty-dishes bucket. The fire smokes patiently.

I mutter an expletive, shove off the wooden bench, and stride out the door.

Gray clouds tear free of the mountain ridge that separates the Southern Patagonian Ice Cap from base camp and race to the east, chased by a terrible wind not felt where I stand. I join Alex, Charlie, Jim, Stefan, and the cast of international suitors to discuss the sudden appearance of our goal. My string of jokes, quips, and curses camouflages my fear.

The Torre emerges from the storm like an enraged angel, sheathed from head to toe in an armor of shimmering rime ice. Clouds swirl around the peak, and afford us brief glimpses of the summit. She looks so evil. Her rewards are elusive and distant, the gauntlet of fear and suffering ever-present and agonizing. Whenever the Torre comes out of her cauldron of cloud and wind we launch a frenzy of backpack stuffing and last-minute eating, choke down a final cup of coffee, and march like lemmings toward her remote fortress, begging for punishment. It is the most extraordinary case of unrequited love.

Donini is readying his assault. Alex is in the hut preparing a meal. I watch spellbound from the clearing and realize that this day their efforts will be wasted. A dark ridge of cloud looms over the ice cap, and within minutes ferocious winds envelop the Torre in a fresh rush of storm. The malignant mountain disappears into the maelstrom and strengthens her icy grip on my heart as she vanishes from view.

•

The stroke of midnight on Christmas Eve catches Alex and me awake, shivering, and spooning in a two-person bivy sack in the ice cave in the Col of Patience a third of the way up the Compressor Route. We chant "merry fucking Christmas" through chattering teeth. Our Christmas present is another stormy retreat down the slopes of Cerro Torre.

Three more weeks pass. Four more times Alex and I trudge the ten miles up the Torre Valley and struggle upward on the slopes of Cerro Torre. Four more times sudden storms ambush us and slam the window of opportunity shut, but only after we have climbed high enough to receive a good dose of pain. We never make it more than one or two rope lengths above the Col of Patience before storms blast us from the walls. I find it hard to contain my desire to act between attempts. I can't let that energy dissipate in unfocused base-camp vibration and frustration, but at the same time I must be careful to keep a fire lit beneath the boiler so that I can summon a new head of steam on demand. Alex and I have been going at Cerro Torre for almost two months. At the same time that I am trying to foster the patience and perseverance to keep battling, I am disappointed, even angry, that we haven't been able to climb the damned mountain yet.

Alex finally runs out of time and returns to the States; his construction business and girlfriend demand attention. Alex isn't the first alpinist to leave Patagonia having dropped all of his savings and months of his time without having stood on a single summit. But I'm still stuck in the trenches below Cerro Torre, and now I lack a partner. I barge into Donini and Stefan's tent: "I'm climbing with you guys now."

Donini is the survivor of four campaigns in the Patagonian Andes. A storm rejected Jim from the summit ridge of Cerro Standhardt when he was attempting its first ascent in 1975. The following year he made the first ascent of Torre Egger with John Bragg and Jay Wilson, a climb that was featured in the pages of *National Geographic*. That success came at the end of a ninety-day campaign, and their climb has never been repeated. Indeed, in the twenty years since, the mountain has been climbed only four other times, each time via a new route. Torre Egger is probably the most difficult summit to attain in the Western Hemisphere. This obstinate spire, with its 9,500-foot summit elevation, makes a mockery of the "Seven Summits" quest worshiped by popular culture. Torre Egger is one of the "Seven Real Summits"—the *hardest* summits on each continent to attain. In 1988, Jim climbed an obscure spire in the Patagonian archipelago with Yvon Chouinard, the founder of the Patagonia brand of outdoor clothing, and sea-kayaked back to civilization. And Donini is here again, twenty-one years after his first trip to the range, in a dogfight with Cerro Torre. Five weeks ago, Donini vowed not to shave until he climbed Cerro Torre, and his grizzly gray beard makes him look like a mountain warrior from the Stone Age.

Some days later the Torre comes out of the storm and stands calm and serene at the head of the valley, ready for battle. We trudge up into the shadow of the beast. In place of a sword, armor, spurs, and a warhorse, I've got ice axes, Gore-Tex, crampons—and Donini. We wallow through thigh-deep snow and finally reach the base of the approach climb that leads to the Col of Patience. The route to the col was hard mixed climbing (a combination of snow, ice, and rock) the first time Alex and I did it, two months ago, and we belayed nearly the entire 1,600-foot distance. But with the familiarity that Jim, Stefan, and I now have, we take few precautions, and with the rope strung out between us, we simul-climb up all but a few steep steps and arrive at the col in the early evening.

From the col the Southeast Buttress rises steeply, and we adapt our tactics to the new terrain. Jim takes the lead, and Stefan belays him. Stefan pays out slack through his belay plate, a simple metal device that will help him hold the rope should Jim fall, while Jim climbs beautiful vertical cracks in the granite. Jim skillfully avoids a few patches of ice that cling to the stone, and every ten or twenty feet he fits a camming device or a stopper into the cracks and clips it to the rope behind him with a carabiner at either end of a nylon sling. These pieces of equipment, known as protection, will shorten any fall Jim might take. Jim reaches a small ledge more than 100 feet above and completes his lead by using a long nylon sling to distribute force equally between several pieces of protection placed within an arm's reach. Jim ties both himself and the lead rope to this anchor, and with the rope thus fixed, Stefan scales it with the aid of two ascenders, hand-sized tools with one-way cams inside that can be pushed up the rope but then catch when pulled down. As Stefan goes up he removes all of the protection that Jim placed so that it can be used again above, and when he gets to the anchor he ties himself to it and fixes my rope. I come up third with the heaviest pack, also using ascenders, but with nothing much to do but enjoy the spectacular view that stretches 100 miles north to Cerro San Lorenzo, shimmering pink in the last fires of the sun.

We suit our tactics to the difficulty of the terrain and to our abilities. On the easiest ground (of which there is very little on Cerro Torre) we climb unroped, risking a fatal fall in order to move as fast as possible. When the terrain gets a bit more difficult, we rope together and climb at the same time—"simul-climbing"—separated by the length of a rope (the standard lengths are 165 feet, 180 feet, and 200 feet). The guy out front periodically places a piece of protection for a little security—although a fall would still likely be injury-producing (but probably not fatal)—and the tail-end-Charlie recovers each successive piece as he climbs past it. When the terrain becomes steeper and more difficult still, we belay each other in turn, first the leader climbing, then the second. Thus we make progress like an inch-worm—the head leads out, then the tail catches up—and the leader places as much protection as he needs (or that is possible to place, as thin or rotten sections of ice or crackless stone are usually unpro-tectable). This inchworm tactic is the one normally employed in the vast majority of climbing: it's the most fun since each partner gets to physically climb the snow, ice, or rock rather than ascend a fixed rope. But on short day climbs close to home there usually isn't a press-ing need for speed, and speed is all-important here in Patagonia. Here we will sacrifice anything—except necessary security measures—for speed, and since it's faster for the second to ascend a fixed rope, espe-cially with a pack, we opt to go with lead-and-fix tactics. "Speed is safety" is one of the oldest alpine saws, and ideally we will climb and descend this peak before the next storm arrives.

We rotate leaders to suit each of our strengths, and also because leading is more engaging—although riskier. We all want to do it. Whoever leads a particular pitch gets to make the most meaningful decisions: where the route goes and how to climb it, how much risk to accept, how to protect the lead, how and where to build the anchors. Our lives depend on these decisions. They must be made—and made well—during every minute of an alpine climb.

Our plan is to climb all night, and hopefully by sunrise we will be in a position from which we can press on to the summit, even in poor weather. I've got more knowledge of the route than Jim or Stefan be-cause of the big push I made with Alex a month ago, so Jim and Stef are going to let me lead through the night. I've spent hours mentally re-hearsing each pitch; I'm sure I can find the route. As the peaks fade into darkness, I pass off the heavy pack, take the lead rope, and climb into the night. There is no moon, just the pool of light projected by my headlamp.

This is not a night for reflection; it is a night for action. As I climb, ice, snow, and stone scroll through the light of my headlamp. I play each new scene before me against my memory of a daylight passage over the same terrain. My crampons scrape over stone. Axe and hammer squeak into hard frozen snow (called névé), crack into ice, and bang off rock. Sparks fly. Occasionally I yell instructions down to Jim and Stefan, but we say little at belays. My world is ice and stone; no view distracts me from the pleasures of climbing. I'm so absorbed by the ascent that I fail to notice the stars as they disappear, one by one, from the night sky.

Gray light seeps into the world from the east as Stefan leads across the hundred-yard bolt traverse. Under clear skies, mountain sunrises are beautiful. Low-angle light from the rising sun cuts across the atmosphere and causes an alpenglow to color the peaks pink, red, and gold—but this is no such spectacular sunrise, just the gray of a creeping dawn. The layer of cloud that slipped in from the west during the night and stole the stars kills the alpenglow. Jim ties into the middle of the lead rope and we simul-climb across the line of bolts. I come over last and remove the slings and carabiners that Stefan used to clip our ropes to the protection bolts. We traverse up and right toward an icy chimney.

Fear has the bile up in my throat, for now that it's daylight I can see the full extent of our exposure. The wall under the bolt traverse plummets down thousands of feet to the glacier. This traverse is reputed to be the part of the route most exposed to bad weather—Alex and I took a tremendous beating here a month ago.

The air is alive with a faint, cold, wet breeze as Jim grunts up the difficult chimney, pounding at the ice and scraping over stone. The weather is obviously deteriorating. Stefan belays at Alex's and my high point. I have nothing to do but worry about the weather. We're in a race with it and with the two Swiss—Thomas Ulrich and Stefan Siegrist—who are hot on our tails and are as committed as we are to pushing through to the top.

For the first time in the eight weeks that I've been trying to climb the peak, the summit of Cerro Torre feels within reach. The return of the west wind is poised to slam us, but we feel that with a determined effort we might just tag the top before the storm develops its full fury. Retreat from up there in a gale will ratchet the danger factor through the roof, but we're game for the risk. If the lords of Patagonia won't give us an opportunity, perhaps we can manufacture one.

Higher, at a belay stance, the three of us build a convoluted tangle of ropes where we change leaders. The two Swiss blitz past us while we fumble with this rope rodeo, and just then Cerro Torre gets hit by the lead phalanx of storm. Angry wind screams around us as we climb onto the Ice Tower, a battlement attached to the side of the peak. We're over halfway up the Southeast Ridge, climbing into the building fury of a Patagonian gale.

Twisted gargoyles of rime ice, condensed directly from the humid atmosphere, decorate the precipitous walls. Clouds swarm around us. Visibility drops to fifty feet. Great rushes of wind careen around the peak with sharp gunfire cracks. The storm drives through the Col of Conquest between Cerro Torre and Torre Egger with the bass growl of a locomotive. Chaotic acoustic effects drive me to the brink of insanity. Cracks and booms heard in the howl of storm are comprehensible to me, but not the mumbled conversations, barking dogs, ringing church bells, and the toneless organ growl that I hear. This aural menagerie seems to belt out the asymphonic chorus that will pipe us into hell.

Then it's my lead, and I force myself to concentrate on the terrain at hand. Beneath a crust of rime, the ice is gray-white and solid. Crampons and axes hold me tight to the slope and furious gusts attempt to buffet me free while I climb past a pair of bulges that push to vertical. The cacophony of sound gnaws at my confidence. Atop a bulge of ice I anchor and fix the rope. The din of storm drowns my shouts. Moments later there are exploratory tugs on the rope before Stefan commits to his ascenders.

A scream sounds from a twisted gargoyle of ice nearby, and suddenly I understand. The mysterious sound effects I am hearing are what climbers call the Patagonian organs—noises produced by the ferocious wind as it crashes and rushes around the gnarled formations of rime. I understand the mechanics of the Patagonian organs, and my fear calms. I laugh and explain the strange acoustics at the top of my lungs to Stefan when he arrives.

Wisps of rime, like goose-down feathers of ice, form on my jacket and bibs, grow on the ropes, and cling to the hardware and slings. The winds swirl and hammer us from all directions. Updrafts fill my jacket with frigid air. With the storm as our constant companion, we encounter several of Maestri's bolt ladders between difficult sections of mixed climbing.

In calm conditions these bolt ladders would be a breeze, but in this storm I fight a frenzied battle for control of my possessed etriers. The wind tosses these portable nylon stepladders in all directions, and updrafts sometimes stream them directly over my head. I have to pull them hand over hand out of the sky and hold them down before I can settle them with the weight of a cramponed boot.

I lead a pitch to the top of the Ice Tower. A gigantic chimney to my left divides the Ice Tower from the bulk of the mountain. Although the core of the Ice Tower is solid granite, ice adheres to the walls that jut out from the main mass of Cerro Torre. Updrafts sweep ice and snow particles up the cleft to my left in the grayish blur of a passing express train. After Stefan joins me, I traverse the peaked roof of the Ice Tower on the side that slopes in toward Cerro Torre's headwall. My heels hang out over the gigantic chimney as I pick and kick my way forty feet horizontally to the left along the roof, aiming for a small saddle. Looking out over the top of the Ice Tower I am actually facing away from Cerro Torre. The view would be spectacular in clear conditions, straight across to Fitzroy and Poincenot, but in this storm I can barely make out the difference between the gray ice in front of me and the gray cloud beyond.

On the far side of the saddle another chimney rises up to divide the Ice Tower from Cerro Torre's East Face. The saddle, at the confluence of the two chimneys, is a maelstrom. The architecture of Cerro Torre channels the chaotic air up to this spot and magnifies the power of the storm. I belay Stefan, then Jim, across to my stance at the point where the ice saddle joins to the base of Cerro Torre's headwall. Behind me, the vertical stone headwall soars up into the storm.

The route rising to our left is running with water. The feeble energy of the sun that penetrates the racing clouds is just enough to melt the rime particles growing on the rock headwall. The struggle up the next eighty feet of mixed ice and rock is one of the hardest leads of my life. I fix the rope to a cluster of Maestri's bolts on a ledge and hug my arms to my chest to preserve precious warmth. While Stefan comes up the rope, I pull the scrunched route "topo" out of my pocket. This line drawing, a sketch map of the route, gives the pitch I just led a very moderate grade, one that I could practically do with a broken leg in normal conditions.

We lumber up the headwall bolts. Stefan leads, and Jim and I ascend the rope. Rime ice grows everywhere. I belay Stefan from a stance high on the headwall and watch Jim push his ascenders up the icy rope below me. Winds swat him from side to side as he pulls up and shoves his top ascender higher. Jim hesitates a second, then his features freeze in terror as he slides ten feet back down the icy rope, neither ascender grabbing the slick rope until friction melts the ice that clogs the cams. Jim cranks quickly up to my stance, the air filled with his invective.

"Jim, look!" A gray shape looms above us, barely visible through the clouds that roar over the top of Cerro Torre. "The summit mushroom. We're close!"

The two Swiss are above a blob of ice plastered smack in the middle of the headwall, on what must be the last rock pitch on the route. Stefan Hiermaier has hung a belay a few feet below the blob and fixed the rope. A strong gust slaps me against Jim and we cuss, awed by the power of the storm; we're tasting the great wind from the wilderness with which the Lord smote down the four corners of Job's house.

"We might make it," yells Jim, "but we're moving so fucking slow!" I fight to get my ascenders attached to the rope as it whips around in the wind.

Periodically I cup each ascender in the hollow of my gloves and breathe on it to unfreeze the cams as I ascend the rope to Stefan. I clip Stefan's belay, and I see that the line of bolts disappears into the ice blob a few feet above. What is this chunk of ice—four feet wide, three feet thick, and about eight feet high—doing stuck right in the middle of this vertical headwall of granite? One of the Swiss stands on top of it and belays.

I dangle below Stefan and shiver while I strap my crampons onto my boots at the dead-hanging belay. I smash into Stefan's legs as the wind screams and tosses us around. God help me if I drop a crampon. But soon I'm ready to tackle that bulge of overhanging ice.

"Be careful!"

My crampons tangle in my etriers as I make a few aid moves to reach the ice. The underside of the bulge overhangs the wall by two feet.

Suddenly, I can't see. The world goes black. I swing from a daisy chain, a nylon leash that I have clipped to a bolt; my crampons scrape against bare granite. I cannot see. "I'm going to die"—the phrase flashes into my brain. The probable consequences of my eyesight calamity are brutally obvious. Yet there's a streak of orange in front of my eyes. Confused, I fight to understand what is wrong. Panic rises. The orange streak tears open a bit. My God, my eyes are frozen shut! I rip my left glove from my hand with my teeth. My axe and glove dangle from my wrist and thrash about madly in the storm. With bare fingers I yank out eyelashes embedded in chunks of rime.

Adrenaline floods through me. I get my gloves back on and top-step my highest etrier, bury my axe pick in the ice, shake my boot loose from the etrier below, and slam my second tool into the ice with no thought to placing protection, just to regaining the bolt ladder above this crazy ice patch. I crank up the bulging ice.

I wiggle a tool free and see Thomas's grin above. "Hook the carburetor!"

"The what?"

"Hook the carburetor!"

Incredulous, I reach my tool up—and it clanks on metal. I pull up and come face-to-face with a large metal object. I heave myself up and stand beside Thomas. It's the only ledge big enough to stand on in the last 500 feet. This contraption, the size of a lawn mower, is Maestri's air compressor, still attached to the headwall twenty-six years after the first ascent. I fix the rope and casually stand on top of the compressor, astounded that someone would bring this huge machine so close to the top of Cerro Torre. The ice that I just climbed is rime that grows suspended from the bottom of the compressor, like an upside-down ice-cream cone.

Stefan arrives atop the compressor. "Do you want us to fix a rope for you?" Thomas asks as he starts to ascend the rope toward his partner above.

"No," Stefan and I shout in unison; we're only 140 feet from the top.

Jim joins us atop the compressor. I lead out five bolts—to where they stop. Maestri smashed his original bolts above this point to prove that the air compressor was essential to his ascent. When American Jim Bridwell did the second ascent of the route in the late 1970s with Steve Brewer, Bridwell hand-drilled a ladder of tiny rivets to pass the section that Maestri destroyed.

A furry layer of gray rime about a quarter-inch thick covers the smooth vertical granite of the headwall. I cannot find the first rivet—which is also gray and about a quarter of an inch thick. The two Swiss rappel past me on their way down from their topmost belay. They've climbed the last pitch of rock, but not the gentle slope of ice and rime that leads to the base of the wildly overhanging summit mushroom. Somewhere up here is a fine line we must not cross. We're the better part of a vertical mile from safety and we must maintain our ability to get down. I scrape more rime feathers from the stone but find nothing.

The roar of the storm as it goes over the top of Cerro Torre is the sound of a jumbo jet with its engines at full power. The clouds are a blur of gray and black-gray fleeing the terrible wind.

Jim yells. I twist to look. His figure is indistinct, though only fifteen feet away. He's gesturing at his wrist. It's late. I look up the last bit of headwall. Even if I climb to the top of this pitch, it still won't feel to me like I've climbed Cerro Torre because that slope of ice would still separate me from the view down the other side (not that we could see anything in this storm). We're at the very upper limit of reason; we've probably got one foot over that line already. If we push on I think we could get there, but I'm not sure we could get back down. We can't afford another step. If we make a mistake up here we will die.

But it's only another 140 feet! "Fuck it, it's just a mountain," I tell myself, and just like that, I abandon ascent and down climb the short bolt ladder to the compressor and join my friends. We may be only 140 feet from the top, but we're nearly 5,000 feet above safety. The rod of the west wind is upon us, and I am suddenly very, very cold.

Stefan asks Jim what he thinks of our chances. Jim yells back, "Survival is not assured."

The descent back to the top of the Ice Tower uses the remaining daylight. We continue down in darkness, using headlamps. After each rappel the wind thrashes the ropes as they fall, but miraculously they never get stuck. Particles of ice whirl around in all directions. Rime grows inside my jacket, and I shiver at the anchors while I wait my turn. Communication is impossible; we decide to rappel based on rope tension. When the rope goes slack, the next person rigs his rappel and goes down.

At the base of the Ice Tower I stand in an icy hell. A barrage of minute ice particles seems immune to the insane winds and exclusively devoted to swarming our stance. Jim and Stefan have their helmeted heads tucked back into their hoods like mutant turtles. We don't exchange a word as we execute the tasks essential to retreat. Past midnight, as I go down first on the last rappel of the traverse, my headlamp flickers and dies. The struggle to maintain the traverse line with the ends of the rope whipping around unseen in the dark is pure terror. At the next stance, below the traverse, I unweight the ropes, secure them, and try, unsuccessfully, to get my light to work.

Moments later, Jim appears out of swirling darkness. "Stefan's headlamp is out, too. We gotta bivy." He attaches the leftover slack of one of the ropes to the anchors and raps down twenty feet. "These stances suck!" he yells up through the storm. "Send down the gear."

I slip the rack of hardware down the rope to Jim. Stefan arrives and immediately switches to the fixed strand of rope and raps to join

Jim. I pull and coil the rappel ropes and go down. Stefan is wedged behind a flake and wriggling his way into his bivy sack. Jim is perched on a small ledge just wider than his skinny butt six feet to the left of Stefan. There must be fifteen pieces of gear in every available nook and cranny—fear has the boys gripped. They saved the biggest stance for me. It's two feet by two feet, covered in a layer of ice, and slopes outward.

The only food left is a lump of cheese. I break it into thirds and share the pieces. Wind rips at my bivy sack as I fish it from my pack. I toss my cheese chunk through the mouth of the sack and worm my way in after it. The wind tears at the sack like machine-gun fire. There's nothing I can do to increase my warmth; I'm already wearing every stitch of clothing I have. I doze and nod and wait for daylight, nibbling at the cheese and shivering uncontrollably. Thankfully, I don't have a light on my watch, so I can't chart the passing minutes.

At dawn, alpenglow shoots under the cloud layer and paints the east faces of Cerro Torre, Torre Egger, and Cerro Standhardt rose red and quiet orange, an Impressionist's masterpiece on a colossal scale. The fury of the storm is spent. Frozen but cheered by the sunshine, we break our bivy and rig for descent. The exposure from our emergency bivy, until now obscured by darkness, is heart-stopping. In daylight, our seats look like good handholds.

We haven't slept in two nights and struggle to maintain focus for the ten rappels that deliver us to the safety of the ice cave. Exhausted by fifty-three hours of consecutive stress, we rest in the ice cave for the morning and early afternoon. The day stays clear and calm. If we had retreated to the cave at the first sign of the previous day's storm and climbed today, we would have cruised to the top in perfect conditions.

•

Stefan and Jim are out of time. They must return to their lives. I have no such pressure—no job, no family, and my budget is holding out—although I have no idea where I'll find the mettle to make another attempt.

My gear is battered, much of it useless. The soles of the new boots I brought to Patagonia two months ago are nearly worn off. My storm bibs are covered in duct tape. My gloves haven't kept my hands dry in six weeks. Even the steel points of my crampons are practically worn off by the mixed climbing the Torre demands. The points that once looked like the tips of daggers now resemble stubby thumbnails.

Jim leaves Patagonia intent on reinventing himself in the wake of his recent divorce with a move from Seattle to Boulder, where I've been based for the last three years. There, he'll temporarily bivy in the house of an old Green Beret buddy, and when I get back from this alpine campaign, we'll find a rental to share. We've known each other for only six weeks, but Patagonia, storm, and Cerro Torre have cemented the foundation of our friendship.

Donini gives me a pile of his equipment as he leaves: bibs, a rope, gaiters, a tent, a dozen pieces of protection to fill the holes in my rack of hardware, and a supply of carabiners—a thousand dollars' worth in all. "Just get on top of the son-of-a-bitch," he says as he boards the bus to leave. My equipment is rejuvenated, but I don't know where to look for more stamina.

Charlie Fowler returns battered from Cerro Torre as Jim and Stefan leave. He has been getting the hammer for almost as long as I have. Since we're the last two Americans still holding the fort in this terrible war of attrition, we join forces. Charlie's casual attitude camouflages an intense drive. He has come to Patagonia often since the late 1970s and has a route on Cerro Catedral in the Paine region and several successes on the Fitzroy massif to show for his efforts. The few months of the year that Charlie isn't traveling, he lives in the little town of Norwood, near Telluride on the western slope of Colorado, and scrapes together his living with a symbiotic combination of guiding, mountain writing, and superb photography. Charlie is one of the most relentless mountain explorers of the last quarter century. If he hasn't been there, chances are that place is flat.

A morning of good weather lures us up to the Torre again, but a fresh rush of cloud stops us from doing any real climbing. We've got a new tactic—a tent and supplies beneath a shelter stone on the immense lateral moraine of the glacier between Cerro Torre and Fitzroy. With this high camp we'll avoid the ten-mile death march back and forth to base camp.

Serious storm lashes the range as we pitch camp, and now we must entertain ourselves during the wait for good weather without the diversions of base camp. Horrified, we discover that *Moby-Dick* is our only book. After dinner I jump to a forty-page lead while Charlie stares at the roof of the tent.

Gusts slap and claw at the tent fabric to wake us in the morning. For the first time in my life I willfully mutilate a book and hand the first chapters to Charlie.

Days later, Charlie and I are immersed in whaling. Sleet, rain, and snow whip our campsite as obsessed Ahab chases the White Whale around the world. Forty-page pamphlets of *Moby-Dick* litter the tent, and the floor is sticky with food spills. Cerro Torre lurks unseen in the storms of Patagonia, as omnipotent and uncaring as Melville's whale.

One morning I snap. Ahab himself provides the precedent: "Ahab and anguish lay stretched together in one hammock, rounding in midwinter that dreary, howling Patagonian cape; then it was that his torn body and gashed soul bled into one another; and in so interfusing, made him mad." Ahab's shipmates had to lace him into a straitjacket and tie him into his hammock until the ship returned to "more sufferable latitudes." Only then did Ahab's delirium, his outward madness, subside. But his soul was never cured; his madness continued to grow inside him, driven and embedded there by the Great White Whale and a Patagonian storm.

"Charlie, we gotta go down. I'm going nuts stuck up here. I need base camp. I need a real meal."

Charlie shrugs his shoulders and soon we are marching down the valley, chased by the wind that hasn't stopped in a week. Four hours later we are laughing, joking, and eating with the members of a Polish expedition sponsored by Pepsi. Wine, whiskey, and stew warms my neglected stomach. It's past midnight when I stumble off to my tent, intending to sleep until noon.

•

"Greg! Greg! Get up. We have to go up. The storm's breaking."

"Oh God . . . you're kidding? What time is it?"

"Five in the morning, and no, I'm not kidding."

I crawl out of my tent and walk to a clearing with Charlie. I stare dumbly at the mountain and pray for storm. Clouds drift through the range but seem to lack the requisite organization and violent purpose.

A cloud swallows the Torre. "Charlie, let's drink some coffee and wait and see what happens."

"I'm sure this is good weather. Those are puff clouds. We should go up."

"I can't face this without coffee."

Charlie goes to his tent to load his backpack. In the hut I slump onto one of the benches made from a split log. The hut is dank and dreary. The ashes in the fireplace are cold.

My mind and body are numb. This isn't the hangover from a single night of swilling whiskey with the Poles. Sixty-seven days of physical and mental strain have precipitated this hangover. I have tried to climb

Cerro Torre, unsuccessfully, thirteen times. With great effort, I fire a stove and set a pot of water to boil.

I did Ranger School when I was in the Army—fifty-eight days with an average of two and a half hours of sleep a night and one meal a day while doing maneuvers designed to simulate combat stress. This Cerro Torre campaign makes Ranger School seem like Boy Scout camp. A great weight burdens my limbs. The energy to try, one more time, to climb this evil mountain eludes me.

The water boils furiously on the stove; jets of steam rise out of the pot, just out of reach. I stare uselessly at the bubbling pot as the minutes tick away. One tremendous sob wracks my exhausted frame. I cannot summon the strength to make coffee.

With a groan that shakes my entire body, I lurch forward and grab the pot of boiling water. Desperately, I want this fool's quest to end, but my only escape is over the top of Cerro Torre.

Charlie returns to find two steaming cups of dark coffee on the stone table in the center of the hut. He'll never know how close our project came to failure over those two brews. We drink cup after cup and check the weather every time we have to leave the hut to relieve ourselves. By nine o'clock I cannot deny the reality of the situation— the weather is good. We need to go climbing.

My mantra is "Please let it end . . . please let it end . . . please let it end" as I stagger over rock rubble on the approach up the dry glacier. The breathtaking scenery of the Torre cirque makes no impression.

Some hours later we load our assault packs with hardware and food at the Norwegian bivy. A fleecy cloud hides Cerro Torre. Consciously, I am amazed we persist, but at some deep level I know Charlie is right—the weather *is* good. These puffy clouds are the clouds of fair weather. Two European parties nearby decide to wait to see what the weather does.

Charlie and I hardly speak as we deal with the climbing to the Col of Patience. There is nothing to discuss. It is late afternoon when we arrive at the ice cave in the col, where we will spend the night. I am done trying to manufacture opportunity. The all-night climbing strategy Jim, Stefan, and I employed two weeks ago only earned us a cosmic ass-kicking.

Enough daylight remains for us to fix our two ropes above the cave to speed progress in the morning. Two Poles from the Pepsi expedition join us in the col and fix their ropes alongside ours. Zbigniew speaks good English, and the four of us arrange ourselves comfortably in the ice cave. I settle into my sleeping bag and eye the roof of the cave. I can do nothing but continue my hope for good weather.

"Zbigniew, how do you say 'good luck' in Polish?"

"*Powodzenia.*"

I chant, "*Powodzenia, powodzenia, powodzenia, powodzenia,*" as the Poles rock with laughter.

Zbigniew fishes a hand-held radio from his pack and babbles in Polish on the radio from the opening of the ice cave. Conversation over, he stashes the radio and goes about preparing dinner.

"What was that all about?" I demand.

"I talk to Polish television."

"What?"

"Yes, I radio to base camp, where we have satellite link. Satellite link goes to live Polish television for Pepsi commercial."

I am astonished. "What did you tell them?"

"That we in ice cave with two crazy Americans, one who chants *powodzenia* like a lunatic. That a storm is raging. That we have no food. No fuel. That if we do not climb this mountain tomorrow we will surely die."

"Zbigniew, that's a total lie."

"Yes, I know . . . but it does not matter."

Worried about the fickle weather and my fading strength, I pass the night listening to the others snore. I want to stand on top of Cerro Torre more than I've ever wanted anything in my life. I watch the pale starlight that filters through the tunnel from the outside world.

·

Neither Charlie's nor my headlamp will work when the alarm detonates predawn. Trapped in blackness, we wake the Poles and send them off while we wait for first light.

An hour later I stand in the col. The stark spires lance into the southern sky. The morning is clear, cold, and windy. I wear all my clothing, and two hats under my helmet. The cold wind snaps at my storm shells. Charlie and I are curt with each other; we are tense and afraid. This wind is laced with menace, and every minute, every move, takes us higher. Both of us know well the terror of storm high on Cerro Torre. Thousands of feet above, the dawn colors the summit ice formations with heavenly light. Charlie and I battle the wind over faces of golden granite, up ridges of snow, and up through chimneys chockfull of ice. A cold blast of spindrift fills my face and glasses. As we approach the bolt traverse, one of the parts of the slender peak most exposed to the capricious Patagonian weather, the wind suddenly drops.

We climb another three or four rope lengths, not wanting to mention the positive change. Eventually Charlie comes up to my stance at the bottom of the Ice Tower and a broad grin spreads across his weathered and lined face. He risks the jinx: "Yeah, man, goin' up." Our tense mood breaks, and we redouble our efforts.

Charlie leads the first few pitches of the Ice Tower and I come up behind. Clouds drift around the peaks and fill the valley, but they don't seem threatening. We climb and watch in wonder as gentle clouds pour around the sides of Cerro Torre, one minute enveloping us in mists before disappearing entirely in the next. I join Charlie at a belay notch just above the point where the two Swiss passed Jim, Stefan, and me on my previous attempt. The notch is a comfortable stance. Here we've just crossed from the east side to the south side of this enormous flying buttress of stone and ice, and I get the view the storm denied us two weeks ago.

Then I couldn't see fifty feet. Now the mists part and I see more than fifty miles. We're three-quarters of the way up, and the whole 7,000 vertical feet of the Torre's South Face drops before my eyes. On the other side of the South Face is the Col of Hope, the high southwest col first reached by Bonatti and Mauri nearly forty years earlier. We're far above the col, so we can see over it, and beyond the col is the vision I've longed for: White upon white streaked with dark gray, the great Southern Patagonian Ice Cap runs out to the far horizon. Ranges of ice and black mountains grow out of the ice cap at the very limit of my perception. Magnificent, the ice desert seems to stretch off into forever.

I return my attention to the myriad tasks of ascent.

Once we're above the Ice Tower and onto the headwall, the clouds clamp around us completely. But the mists are still. As I change a roll of film, a scream of pain and the whoosh of an unseen object falling through the mist shatters my concentration. Two agitated voices shout back and forth, echoing down from the murk above.

"Someone's hurt," Charlie hollers down. We continue up the bolt ladder toward the mishap. Suddenly the ends of two ropes appear, and the Poles join Charlie at a stance above. I have no clear idea of what is happening. I cannot hear the conversation. What has gone wrong? Do they need help?

The Poles are indistinguishable in their matching windsuits covered with Pepsi logos. They pull their ropes and prepare to rappel again. Charlie helps them rig and tries to stay out of the way. A Pole raps past me. It's Zbigniew. He stops and tells me that he was leading up the ice to the top of the compressor with his partner belaying fifteen feet below. Zbigniew topped out on the compressor, clipped himself off, leaned back, and kicked his left foot out to the side for balance. His foot dislodged a flake of yellow granite the size of a tabletop, four feet long, three feet wide, and three inches thick. The tabletop fell, smashed the elbow of his partner, and then disappeared into the mists below. His friend's elbow is useless, Zbigniew tells me, but there is no blood. They refuse help, rappel, and are soon swallowed by the mist, doing proud the reputation of Eastern European hardmen.

Shaken, Charlie and I continue upward. Only the fact that that chunk was tabletop-shaped, so it could Frisbee off into space, saved us. If it had been more of a block, it would have plummeted straight down and crushed us.

The massive bulk of Cerro Torre's summit mushroom looms out of the cloud. Charlie straps on his crampons and leads the ice-cream cone of rime pegged to the bottom of the compressor. I clamp my ascenders to the rope after he fixes it and go up to join him. The only two pitches of this mountain I haven't previously climbed are before me. Charlie hands me the rack, sends me out onto the last pitch of rock climbing, and says, "Slay this white whale."

Up I go into the cloud, stretching between rivets. Some hook moves, a few funky pitons, rivets, and a free move get me to the last anchor, within easy distance of the top. This pitch, which I found impossible in the storm with Jim and Stefan, doesn't seem too hard today. Charlie comes up to join me; his crampons grind against the granite. Charlie leads the last pitch of low-angled ice up to a small plateau at the base of the ice mushroom. There is not a breath of wind. I ponder our coming night descent and spontaneously yell up at Charlie, barely seen in the mist, "Let's spend the night on top!"

My idea seems crazy and impossible, but there is no wind—we could light a match in this calm. I fight to get my crampons on as Charlie establishes a belay up top. I climb to join him, overwhelmed with relief at having accomplished what I set out to do sixty-eight days and fourteen attempts ago. Charlie and I hug and laugh and grin and vow to spend the night in a foxhole-like crevasse we discover at the base of the summit mushroom. The mushroom doesn't look possible. A five-foot overhang of rime, like the eaves of a roof, blocks access to the very top. It stings not to stand on the true summit and crown this climb with an absolute success. I'm going to have to live with those few untrodden meters looming over my memory of the summit of Cerro Torre.

We prepare our ropes and backpacks to insulate us from the ice beneath, and I cannot force the grin from my face, despite the horrible risk that a storm will rage ashore and catch us at maximum distance from safety. We squirm into our bivy sacks with nothing but a few cookies and a pint of Tang to share. I shiver all night without a sleeping bag, but the outrageousness of our aerie warms my soul. We laugh and talk and doze and wait for the dawn. Gentle breezes waft the clouds from the sky.

Shivering, we emerge from our icy nest as the first streaks of red and orange color the eastern horizon. My eyes sweep the dark skies—stars twinkle everywhere in the velvet night. Not a single cloud mars the vault of southern sky. Mountain shapes form in the black-gray light before dawn. I fumble with crampon straps by the light of my headlamp. Pure cold pierces my fingers, but with my crampons fastened to my boots I can safely wander around the Torre's summit plateau.

In awe and anticipation I stagger to my feet, grab an ice axe, and thirst for the sunrise. High in my alpine world, I have no link to the modern world below. My connection to campfires and conversation, sleeping bags and warmth, food and sustenance, lovers and friends is lost. I have passed from the civilized world into a world of raw power, boundless possibility, infinite sky, impossible color, tremendous size, and utter, overwhelming silence.

The orange stain spreads along the eastern rim of the world. Nearly 10,000 feet below, desert steppes sunk in blackness stretch away and merge with the orange to the east. Color creeps into the sky, and the black vault overhead stains deep purple. Behind us, to the north, west, and south, lies the vast expanse of the Southern Patagonian Ice Cap. Great unknown mountains rise from that savage frozen sea. The approach of the sunrise tints the ice peaks pink, light purple, and blue.

Only our giddy laughter and the crunch of our crampons on the frosty crust breaks the silence, discordant noises swallowed without echo by the great beautiful void. The reality of the moment is so much more than the summit we strove for.

A touch of yellow washes the orange east. A pause. For one precious instant the world catches its breath, and then, with a flash, the sun breaks the horizon. Vibrant, pulsing gold blazes on the peaks, ridges, rock, ice, and snow as the first rays of the rising sun touch the spires of the Patagonian Andes. A crown of gold shimmers on the mushroom of rime ice over our heads. In a brilliant instant my future and past compress into the crystal sunrise. Ecstasy and beauty overwhelm me, and with outstretched arms I greet the sunrise. I have done what I set out to do.

The glory lasts only a moment. The sun loses his tenuous hold on the eastern horizon and lifts free. The golden hues vanish. The sun pales to yellow and rises into the morning. A new day is born and the Patagonian Andes gain their stark daytime contrasts: black, gray, brown, yellow, and brilliant, piercing white.

Reality returns. Charlie and I are a long, long way from our futures. Fortune has blessed us with eleven windless hours on the summit of Cerro Torre, but we cannot remain. Storms surely lurk under the western horizon. We organize our descent. One last time I tromp over to the western edge of the summit and gaze down onto the ice cap. The black shadows of the Torres are etched like fangs onto the white ice below. I wish Alex, Jim, and Stefan were here to share these shadows, that sunrise, and this pellucid sky. Only by standing on their shoulders have I been able to get here.

Charlie belays me down to the top of the headwall. Before I slither over the edge to clip the anchor I look up to the absolute top of Cerro Torre. There it is, still a few yards over Charlie's head, the place I wasn't good enough to get.

"Doesn't make much difference," I tell myself. "Besides, you can always come back."

I turn away and rig the ropes for descent.

On the way down, a circling condor shares our celebration. We rappel through three parties of Europeans; six of the seven climbers are on their way to the summit of Cerro Torre on their first attempt. I am incensed that they can climb the Torre so easily, when I have suffered so monstrously for the same end.

Then my anger mellows. I may have put my heart and soul on the line for sixty-eight days and made fourteen attempts to climb Cerro Torre, but I accomplished nothing significant in the larger scheme of mountaineering. Maestri's Compressor Route has been climbed dozens of times. The only importance of this ascent is its importance to me, and my Cerro Torre will never be the same mountain that it is to those who make the summit so easily.

•

The good spell that got Charlie and me to the top of the Torre lasted a week. A few pathetic impulses of storm flushed through the range, but the atmospheric pressure never dropped off its high plateau. By great good fortune, my girlfriend, Robyn, arrived the very day we got down from the Torre. Charlie left Patagonia in the aftermath of a classic summit celebration with the two Poles, Robyn, and a pair of other Americans, John Catto and Peter Gallagher—old friends of Charlie's and new friends of mine—who had topped out on Aguja Poincenot.

In the next days, Robyn and I climbed Media Luna and de la "S," two of the lesser towers—I fueled only by the fumes of Cerro Torre—before the pressure fell through the floor, the range disappeared in storm, and the skies let loose Noah's deluge. Robyn wanted to hang around in the hopes that we could do one more climb, and I tried to be game, but in truth, I couldn't have cared less, and as long as the storm continued I would not be forced into action. Even carrying our gear down from base camp seemed too big an obstacle to confront. The west wind drummed fat drops of rain against the tent. Each morning I splashed through puddles to the hut and rebuilt a fire from the last night's dying embers. In the dark hut under slate gray skies I dodged leaks and listened to the plastic walls and roof flap in the wind. I couldn't summon the strength to read. I could barely link thoughts together. I met some people and heard a few stories, but of those days I have virtually no memory. Day followed dank, dreary day. I stoked the fire with wet wood and sat and suffered as the hut filled with smoke. I remember the yellow-orange logs burning and smoking, the black charcoal, the white ashes, the simple warmth of the fire. Nights I sat in the hut with the fire, spilled wine into my empty cup, and did nothing as rats pillaged our food stash. Mornings I mixed the first pour of coffee with the last drops of wine. I remember my feet up on the stone table. I felt like a battlefield, the battle fought, the field not yet cleared of dead. The wind broke great branches off the beech trees around camp, fresh wreckage in the war between life and Patagonia. The marrow had been sucked out of my bones and replaced with lead. The slightest thoughts of movement took fifteen minutes to foment into action. Conversation taxed my concentration. The fire was my only solace, and I watched tongues of flame consume brand after brand. I'm sure I was a poor companion, but I don't really remember.

¡Que siga la tormenta! My fondest hope was that the storm would continue forever, that I would not be called upon to crush myself against the walls of another Patagonian titan. I felt like I had crossed a stormy sea or staggered out of a waterless desert. How much more battering I could have stood I do not know——and I don't want to know. I had done what I set out to do, that seemed something, and for once, it was enough.

The storm raged for twenty days and more. I never did see the end of it, either. Robyn disturbed my inertia and decided we should head far north to Bariloche and fair-weather rock climbing. I followed willingly enough. Our bus bounced out of the mountains alongside the tormented waters of Lago Viedma under a scudding sky. Of Cerro Torre, wrapped in storm behind us, there wasn't the slightest trace.

I owned nothing but a pile of battered climbing equipment, a point-and-shoot camera, a bag of exposed film, and a journal full of barely coherent scribbling. I had just enough money in my wallet to take me rock climbing in Bariloche, give me a brief stay in Buenos Aires, and get me home to Colorado. The total monetary value of my life could be earned in a few days of casual labor. Some of my fellow West Point graduates earn that much in an hour. But no place on earth sells what I took away from Patagonia. No money buys the friendship and respect of an Alex Hall, a Charlie Fowler, a Stefan Hiermaier, or a Jim Donini. I had not been found wanting, and I had seen the heart of the sunrise. I left Patagonia a rich man.

ASCENTS, DESCENTS, SUMMITS, AND THE NATURE OF ALPINISM

A RHYTHM OF ASCENT AND DESCENT GOV-
erns the alpine existence. Like swells over a deep ocean, rise
follows fall follows rise in majestic procession. Alpine ascents
and descents possess a similarly mysterious imperative, for
who can fathom the tides that move a man? Ascent and descent, rise and fall—to the uninitiated they seem to trace the
endless graph of a sine wave. But the ascents and descents of
an alpinist differ from each other in the same way that no two
sunrises, nor pair of sunsets, are ever alike.

Generally speaking, ascents and descents can be divided
into two broad categories: good and bad. And the distinction
has nothing to do with whether or not a summit is reached in
between.

A good ascent is a victory. A good ascent can be a summit
well won under a blue sky; or it can be like the fight of an over-
matched boxer, whose victory is the courage to step into the
ring and struggle on as long as possible. History, however, seldom records such triumphs of heart. Thus it is with an alpinist, whose greatest achievements and most remarkable

statements of character are often played out in losing efforts and doomed causes. Failure is part of the game, and failure can be magnificent, for it is often harder *not* to climb a mountain than it is to climb it. At the other end of the failure spectrum are excuses, like cases of the "Torre knee" or the "Fitzroy stomach," two common gripes that appear when the weather improves. Such piddling excuses have little to do with an honest recognition that one is not yet equal to the task, and nothing whatsoever to do with the fever that grabs an aspiring alpinist at the slightest hint of improving weather.

A good ascent is a small party traveling light and fast on a big mountain equipped with the simple tools of the alpine trade: a few ropes, some hardware, crampons and ice axes, a little food and water, clothing, and camping gear. Nothing more, and often less. A good ascent rises to meet a mountain's difficulties. Good ascents are those that are made in "alpine style," without a succession of well-stocked camps and without an excess of fixed ropes to speed progress over a mountain's difficulties, to assist in the ferrying of supplies between camps, or to secure descent. Alpine-style ascents are made without the use of guides and support personnel, and they go up and down in one bang.

Bad ascents reduce a mountain's challenge with such techniques, and they are what is called "expedition-style" climbs. Mankind's voyages to the moon show that we can overcome any obstacle with vast resource expenditure. There is no need to prove the same point in the mountains. Alpinism is not about just getting to the top of some geographic feature, it's about climbing that feature well. Mountains deserve our best efforts. Otherwise, alpine endeavor degenerates into the squalor of a construction site. What construction there is in alpinism—the construction of an efficient system of protection with rope and hardware—is most elegant when it is a temporary construction soon dismantled by an ascending second. Thus climbers leave little trace as they ascend a great mountain. Done well—with balance, with discipline, courage, skill, mental mastery—a climb becomes an ascent. An alpinist strives to do more with less, and stands taller by virtue of what he has chosen to do without. Alpinism is one aspect of human endeavor where more, done with more, is definitely less. Bad ascents are the victories of an army, albeit a small one, and a defeat for alpinism. The soul of alpinism is to travel light and fast through a dangerous landscape in pursuit of a personal star. That is ascent.

Like ascents, descents are also characterized as good or bad, but it doesn't take an informed eye to appreciate the difference. More accurately, descents are either controlled or uncontrolled. A controlled descent is survived unscathed; the other kind is not, and death is the ultimate alpine failure.

Although it's easy to comprehend, controlled descent from a big mountain is not easy to execute. In descent we stand with real danger; we are past the engagement of ascent, past the elation of the summit, or both. We are hungry and thirsty and sleep deprived. Often, there is storm. Our margin of safety is thinnest. Woe unto the alpinist who has squandered the last of his strength to get to the top. The reserves needed to get down are an alpinist's bridge to the future. Mountains rarely forgive mistakes made in descent.

Summit moments stand apart. There are few summits in life, and even fewer in the alpine life. But the success of the alpine life isn't measured in summits, and summits aren't the proper place to celebrate a successful ascent, either. A successful ascent should be celebrated in the warmth, comfort, and safety of a bar or tent far from the mountain's dangerous embrace. Not to imply that summits are insignificant, just that they can't be fully appreciated without survival and perspective.

Summits. You want to get there so badly, but once you do, nothing happens. There is no band playing. You climb up and all of a sudden you can see down the other side. But there is no great spiritual revelation that automatically goes along with the view, and a certain part of me even resents the summit. Something truly beautiful—the ascent—is gone forever, past, and can never be recaptured. My Patagonian summit memories aren't the alpine memories that stand tallest for me. My memories of ascent do that; climbing a difficult section of rock or ice, the great peaks around me, my attention laser focused, the issue of the summit in doubt, and the weather on the cusp of a change.

Ironically, these are precisely the moments I try consciously to avoid. If I were more of a man I'd say: Give me the wild, insecure moments when fear has the bile up in my throat, when desire sits like a lead weight in my gut, and when the summit is maybe, just maybe within reach. But I don't have the courage to ask for those moments. Each time up I hope, I beg, for an easy climb. I hope to climb and descend without hassle, without fear, without storm. But I know that I am the best man I can ever hope to be in precisely those moments of maximum fear and doubt.

A summit ends all that. A summit takes the song of ascent out of my veins. On a summit we stop, do some sightseeing, share some water and food if we've got any, then go down. My secret desire has never been to stay on the summit forever. My secret desire is to be locked forever onto the cutting edge of an ascent.

•

Alpinism is so simple: dream about the mountain, go to the mountain, see the mountain, go up the mountain, come back down the mountain, go home. So simple, yet so extraordinarily complex.

The Alps are the birthplace of the sport, and in the old days climbing was all about reaching summits. But the modern climbing world has splintered into many different specialties and subspecialties. There are rock climbers who never get cold and big-wall climbers who scale cliffs that take days to surmount. There are ice climbers and sport climbers, aid climbers, peak baggers, free climbers, soloists, and competition climbers. There are climbers who never venture more than a few hundred feet—horizontally or vertically—from their cars, and there are climbers who do little besides talk. All, in their own ways, are climbers.

Alpinists are the all-rounders of the climbing game, for alpinism is not a specialist's endeavor. Alpinists must cultivate a working knowledge of all facets of climbing, and the alpinist's is a long apprenticeship. It takes years to acquire these skills. Most of the rewards of climbing—in coin or in glory—go to the kings and queens of each particular specialty. The alpinist is the jack-of-all-trades, master of none, and tangible rewards elude him. And that is a good thing, because the extreme danger of alpinism makes the quest for coin and glory a zero-sum game. Those who climb for the wrong reasons, or choose to press on for the wrong reasons, or select objectives for the wrong reasons are very, very likely to end up dead.

Grades and numbers measure the progress and relative abilities of the specialists, and the numbers lend themselves to public appreciation and comparison. The hardest this, the most extreme that. There is some truth in such statistics, but they tell a soulless story. There are few relevant quanta in alpinism.

Modern alpinists play out their game on steep mountains. Difficulty interests the alpinist, who doesn't necessarily seek the easiest way to the top. An alpinist cuts the cord with the safety and security of the world below and ascends into the unknown, sometimes literally on an unclimbed route or, more often, figuratively as one begins an inner exploration. The game is at its best when both occur. Doubt is crucial to alpinism, and an ascent lacks a cutting edge if its outcome is certain from the beginning. There is little honor in certain success, but there is much to be gained from a probable failure. Facing doubt, and its companion, fear, an alpinist ascends.

It may come as a surprise to learn that falling isn't the greatest danger for an alpinist. Each individual climber has control of that, and he or she can always retreat if faced with a section of climbing that is too difficult. Climbing is a control sport, and the greatest dangers are the "objective dangers" that we cannot control: weather, falling objects, and, to a lesser degree, descent. Bad weather can freeze us to death, blow us away, cause buildups of ice and snow that can avalanche, or make us so damn uncomfortable that it fuels a stupid decision that starts a lethal chain of mistakes. Strangely, weather that's too good can kill us as well, for an extended good spell with warm temperatures will cause snow, ice, and loose rocks to fall. Intuition culled from long experience is the card we play against the things we cannot control, and the best alpinists I know trust their gut feelings.

A combination of beautiful summit and beautiful line lures an alpinist to a given mountain, and such beauty eludes statistical definition. Beautiful summits come to fine points, and the lines that rise to those tops can be obvious features—like a huge ridge or a soaring buttress or a white-gray sheet of steep ice that clings to an entire face— that draw the eye (practiced alpine eye or otherwise) from miles around, or a line can be a link-up of discontinuous cracks and ephemeral ice smears, subtle features that only experience can thread up a mountain. The best lines are steep, beautiful, difficult, and relatively unmenaced by the threat of falling debris, and an alpinist will travel to the other side of the world and walk a month to attempt a line that has caught his fancy.

There is no single, ultimate alpine venture. For me, there will be no crowning triumph, no final victory, no perfect summit. I do not expect to find the holy city. I am not a paradise person. There is nothing I want there. Warm sun, shade, a full belly, and cool waters serve only to spark dreams of new mountains. I cannot abide the thought of a flat existence. Some self-knowledge is all that we can hope for from life, and it is no small thing. Whatever small measures of it I've accumulated have come from the mountains.

Fear and infinite natural power are our adversaries, hope and will our strongest arms, and endurance our only glory. Alpine beauty is deceptive—it's ruthless, painful war up there. I do not know if climbing makes me a better man. I have no certain evidence, but I hold fast to the hope that it does, and in the name of that hope I have abandoned much of everyman's existence.

Mountains aren't worth dying for, but they are worth risking dying for. Make no mistake, my alpine goal is to die in bed, old, laughing and smiling and talking trash with my last breath, having lived a lifetime of good ascents and controlled descents, perhaps peppered with a few more summits, perhaps not, before I undertake that final, inevitable expedition. I hope I find mountains there, too.

THIS BOOK MAY OPEN WITH ACCOUNTS OF AS-
cents, descents, and summits on Cerro Torre, sorcer-
ess supreme of the Patagonian Andes, but my alpine story
doesn't begin there. My story begins, if any story can ever
be said to truly have a beginning, eleven years before, on
a warm September Saturday afternoon in 1985 on the side
of Storm King Mountain, in New York, one of the mountains that rise from the Hudson River above fortress West
Point. The leaves were just beginning to turn. I was nineteen, a cadet at the military academy, and I had followed my
roommate—who claimed climbing experience and had the
rope, harness, and hardware to prove it—to the base of a cliff
band of dark rock to get a taste of climbing. As cadets, Brian
and I were an awkward mix of soldier and college student subject to West Point's ceaseless regime. Both of us had survived
the frontal assaults of plebe year unscathed, but now chafed
against the military rub in our second year. Brian made climbing sound exciting, and I was game to try anything that promised relief from the academy grind. What I didn't realize at the

time (and in Brian's defense, neither did he) was that the sum total of Brian's climbing experience, a weekend climbing course at the University of Utah twenty-four months before, was perhaps worse than no experience at all.

The night before, we'd spread the climbing gear out on our room's linoleum floor. The rope, harnesses, slings, carabiners, hexes, and saddle wedges that Brian had signed out from the Cadet Mountaineering Club's equipment locker made an impressive display. Brian showed me how to put on a harness and tie a figure-eight knot and gave me a class in the fine art of the belay. There are few truly reliable things in life, but the figure-eight knot is one of them. I have tied a figure eight thousands of times in the last fifteen years; it's a climber's staple. I make it, I make it right, and it does exactly what I expect, every time, without exception, and if I ever fail in the small discipline of tying that knot properly, I don't expect to survive. But made right, the figure eight is a thing of simple and functional beauty. Climbing is for those who can cover the details.

We uncoiled the rope onto the boulders and fallen leaves beneath the trees at the base of the dark cliff, and each of us tied into an end. I put Brian on belay. He slung the rack over his shoulder and climbed into a vegetated gully that split the cliff band while I dealt out the string behind him. He pulled aside greasy vines to uncover dirty handholds. Loose rocks, dirt, and plant fragments rained down as Brian struggled upward. I slowly paid out the rope while Brian worked his way up a hundred feet of unclimbed stone. At a shelf, Brian knotted himself to a stout bush, shouted, and I undid the belay device. Brian recovered what slack remained and rigged a belay for me. My turn to climb.

I peeled off my T-shirt, rolled it up, tucked it into my shorts, and climbed up the grimy gully toward Brian. Sweat slicked my torso. Above the treetops the view opened out onto the Hudson where its gray waters slide down into the narrow reach between Storm King Mountain and Breakneck Ridge. A speedboat whined past on the water below, its load of Saturday pleasure seekers oblivious to the minor drama playing itself out over their heads. Also averted were the keen eyes of West Point's authorities. I buzzed with a sublime cocktail of fear and adrenaline.

We scaled pitch after pitch and the shadow cast by Storm King stretched out over the water. We had no food, no water, and no certain knowledge of how to safely descend, but we climbed on. The great shadow reached the Hudson's far shore. The angle of the cliff lessened as we neared the top. The shadow gained the houses and hilltops beyond the river. We reached the trees at the top of the cliff band as darkness fell.

The night was black, without moon, and we had no flashlight. We wandered around in the dark for a while, but we were constantly afraid that the next step would plunge us over the edge of the 500-foot cliff we had taken all day to climb. We were treed like house cats. Up there, hungry and thirsty, and utterly in the dark, we made our one truly good decision of the day: We decided not to descend at night. Clad in our gym uniforms—shorts, T-shirt, socks, and tennis shoes— Brian and I snuggled into a nest of vines and brush, piled leaves on our legs and torsos to keep warm, and dozed until dawn. With the new day, we discovered a straightforward descent slope without trouble, scrambled down, and dashed back to the barracks. We hadn't been authorized to spend the night out, and we had no doubt that there would be consequences.

We returned early Sunday morning to a quiet barracks and reported to our company's weekend CCQ, the cadet in charge of quarters, who happened to be our good friend Steve Brophy. Brian, Steve, and I were in a pickle hard to appreciate by anyone who hasn't been subject to the West Point honor code. The honor code simply states that "a cadet shall not lie, cheat, or steal, nor tolerate those who do." And the code is for real at West Point; it's not the pony-show honor code occasionally pulled out of the stable and paraded around by some universities. Cadets live it, and they are punished for violating it— almost always with expulsion.

For example, in four years, I was never aware of another cadet cheating on a test. I'm quite certain that it never happened in my presence, and this in classrooms that almost never had any kind of proctor in the room during tests. Once, during a history WPR (written partial review, as midterms are called at West Point), the professor handed out the tests and promptly disappeared to his office downstairs. We then watched in stunned silence as a guy at the front of the room pulled his books out from under his desk and flipped to the relevant chapters. My gut clenched as I tried to face the fact that I'd have to report this guy if I didn't want to be considered a cheat along with him. Fortunately, a more intelligent classmate leaned forward: "John, this is a closed-book test." The poor fellow went white as death, and not a thought in a dozen minds was on Korean War military policy.

"Oh, shit," gasped John, frozen by the enormity of his transgression. Then he bolted from his desk and disappeared downstairs to the offices of the history department, frantically searching for our professor so that he could confess. Minutes later he was back to clear his desk. The instructor, an Army captain, recognized John's honest mistake and his honorable handling of the situation and allowed him to take a different version of the test at a later hour. The honor code, far more than the uniform, is what sets West Point apart.

Steve Brophy, as that weekend's CCQ, knew we were out rock climbing, but he did not know whether we were officially authorized to spend the night out doing it. Brian and I could have easily evaded punishment by telling Steve that we were allowed the night out. Steve would have taken us at our word and that would have been the end of it. But both Brian and I knew for a God-given fact that we were *not* authorized the night out, and to say otherwise would be a lie. So we told Steve the truth straight up, and he found himself in the unenviable position of setting the wheels of military justice in motion against us.

Midmorning Monday Brian and I stood on the carpet in front of our company tactical officer's desk awaiting punishment. But in the meantime, the climbing gods had meted out another brand of justice. Angry rashes had erupted on my arms, legs, and face. All those greasy vines we had climbed through and slept in had been poison ivy. As we stood stiffly at attention and explained our delinquency, the blisters on my thighs were blossoming to the size of quarters. I could hardly endure our wool uniform pants.

Brian and I were both tortured by the desire to fidget and scratch. Our offenses were grievous: We had signed out and not returned at the prescribed time and we had not been authorized to spend the night away from the barracks. We could have easily lost what few privileges yearlings (sophomores) have for the remainder of the semester. But Major Fields was lenient, because he could see that we had exercised good judgment and not forced our way down in the dark at risk of the fatal pitch. What was perhaps not so obvious to a lay observer was that the entire enterprise had been a staggering exercise of bad judgment. As it was, Major Fields gave us a "slug" (as goes the cadet slang) that cost us our freedom for the next two weekends. We both felt lucky; we could rightly have been handed a much more serious punishment.

Brian and I were lucky to get away with that bold and ignorant foray up 500 feet of unclimbed rock, utterly dependent on equipment we barely knew how to use. The number of firsts that I rang off that day made no impression: first climb, first fall, first lead, first lead fall, first first ascent, first open bivouac. The photos we took that day document many egregious mistakes. But the climbing gods smiled, and we paid for none of our incompetence and inexperience in blood. We survived, and despite the miseries of restriction and poison ivy, I couldn't wait to climb again.

The military academy might seem like an odd place to find a guy hell-bent for the Patagonian Andes, but exactly the same fire motivates me today that motivated me to attend West Point in the first place— the desire to lead a unique and adventurous life. Life at West Point certainly was unique; adventurous it was not. They don't call 'em uniforms for nothing. How ironic that in a casual foray conceived to break the monotony of military academy life, I determined the future course of my life.

My metamorphosis wasn't immediate, but within one year of my uneducated trip up the side of Storm King, the one-word description I used to describe myself was *climber*. I survived at West Point, but I lived to climb. I spent every minute I could spare away from the demands of West Point clinging to the side of a cliff.

One of the best things about West Point was its location. The Shawangunks, a premier East Coast climbing destination, are only about forty miles away. There are more than a thousand separate rock climbs on the walls of "the Gunks," near New Paltz, and the crags are steeped in climbing history. I've loved history ever since I was a small boy, and I've always been enthralled by stories of explorers and engineers, artists and adventurers, soldiers, sailors, scientists, and scoundrels. That love was another strong magnet that had pulled me to West Point, for West Point is a wellspring of history. As I immersed myself in the climbing scene, a whole new type of history cracked open for me. Climbing history is a dazzling collection of characters and stories, and many of my new climbing heroes—people like Fritz Weissner, Kevin Bein, Mike Freeman, Henry Barber, Steve Wunsch, and John Bragg—made lasting marks on the vertical and overhanging cliffs of the Shawangunks. Their hard-core experiences seemed light-years removed from mine, but the climbing rope is a thread that runs through time as well as space, and I tried to live up to their bold and excellent examples.

I would return to West Point on a Sunday night exhausted by a weekend foray to the Gunks, having battled climbs with names like Stirrup Trouble, the Stand, Cheap Thrills, Never Never Land, Sound and Fury, High Exposure, and Crash and Burn. My classmates would return from a weekend quest to Vassar, Smith, Yale, Dartmouth, or New York City, having indulged in drunken attempts to meet and seduce girls—in most cases with a monumental lack of success. Tilting at stone windmills in the Shawangunks, pushing myself hard, seemed charged with meaning not found in the hedonistic pursuits of my classmates.

Soon Patagonia began to seize terrain in my consciousness. I suppose I first became aware of the word *Patagonia* soon after I started climbing, but only as the name of a popular brand of outdoor clothing. In my quest to expand my climbing knowledge in any way possible, I gobbled up the classics of climbing literature. I read about historic ascents in the Alps, Yosemite, the Scottish Highlands, and about expeditions to the high peaks of Asia. I pored over technical manuals that discoursed on climbing technique, and when I started to ice climb I bought *Climbing Ice,* a how-to book by pioneer climber Yvon Chouinard. In one anecdote, Chouinard ventures with four friends to the southern tip of South America—to a place called Patagonia. Patagonia was a *place*! Chouinard writes of near-ceaseless storm, magnificent peaks, months of struggle, and of a sparkling instant spent atop Cerro Fitzroy. Some years later, when Yvon needed to name his new outdoor clothing company, the word he chose to express his ultimate vision of hard-core was *Patagonia*. I read that vignette again and again while I sat in my West Point cell, the layout of which was precisely regulated by the Barracks Arrangement Guide. Those rooms were so spartan that my memories of them are in black and white. There, as I was surrounded by uniforms and texts on mechanics, military history, thermofluid dynamics, and electrical engineering, Patagonia shone like a beacon from another world. I read Chouinard's story over and over, until I knew every detail. One day, I told myself, I will climb there. But I was also smart enough to know that if a historic badass like Chouinard wrote in such low and respectful tones of Patagonian difficulties, then I was a long way from being able to handle them.

To know the relative nature of time, one needs only to know the grind of West Point's second and third years. During those years the military lost what hold it had on my passions. One of my classmates was obsessed by sleep. "Think about it," he used to say. "If you sleep twelve hours a day you only spend two years at West Point." The combats of plebe year and my romantic adolescent visions faded into the realities of life in uniform. I felt like I was getting nothing done. I've never felt more lonely than I did at West Point, despite being in constant contact with close friends. The lack of privacy is astonishing, and no cadet is ever free from intrusion. None of the barracks rooms have locks, so anyone can barge in without warning. My defense was mental retreat. I conjured up private worlds, a technique I practice to this day. I could pay enough attention to the world around me not to make an utter fool of myself, but in the rest of my mind I was gone, tasting a windswept world where clouds swirled around enchanted peaks. Nobody ever touched that world, and even today, nobody ever does. That corridor of consciousness where imagination and ambition merge is one of my most prized possessions, the seat of whatever power I possess.

And I climbed. Between classes, or once drill or intramural sports were over in the afternoon, I changed into my gym uniform, grabbed my climbing shoes, and dashed to an out-of-the-way (and largely out-of-view) retaining wall constructed of blocked-together granite that connects the dean's office to Mahan Hall. There, traversing the 200-

foot-long Dean's Wall never farther than five feet above a grassy land-
ing, I found freedom. Clinging to that stone wall, absorbed in the
physical and mental discipline of climbing, I was free from military
rigors, unaware even of the uniform on my back; I was master of my
own time and space. I spent practically every weekend that I was allowed to leave West Point at the Shawangunks, and every spare minute
during the week I clambered across the Dean's Wall. If I had a bad day
I would run to the Dean's Wall, even in midwinter, and traverse until
all sensation was gone and my fingers were dead white. Without
climbing, I don't think I would have graduated. My morale would not
have been able to stand it.

I must have thought about quitting West Point a million times. I
knew I'd be happier out of uniform, but happiness doesn't motivate
me. I've never much been drawn by the promise of heaven. There are
no uncertain outcomes in paradise. I love the highs and lows of life,
and I also felt that in my early twenties, I didn't have the perspective to
make such a momentous life decision. In the end, it simply might have
been my desire to finish what I start that kept me at West Point. That
and my fear of failure, of being a quitter. But the paradigm shift that is
so apparent with almost fifteen years of perspective wasn't so obvious
while it was happening, so I stuck it out at West Point. All I knew at the
time was that I was chained and depressed in uniform and unfettered
and alive when I climbed. I felt as if I were living two parallel lives.

I got my first taste of real mountains when the Cadet Mountaineering Club made a winter trip to the Highlands of Scotland. In the
Scottish winter, steep ice-choked gullies split dark mountain walls
hammered by North Atlantic gales. None of the summits touch 5,000
feet, but the climbing is bold and cold. I didn't know it at the time, but
Scotland gave me two cornerstones of my future Patagonian obsession: a love of low-altitude mountaineering and a taste for stupen-
dously bad weather.

Between my cow and firstie (junior and senior) years I flew to California and began a cross-country climbing trip with the three weeks of leave I had allotted between my military duties. I trucked my way generally eastward from my hometown of Goleta, California, and climbed in Idyllwild; Las Vegas; Salt Lake City; City of Rocks, Idaho; Boulder, Colorado; and in the Needles of South Dakota. I squeezed every possible second out of my Needles time and drove to New York in one terrible, sleepless push. I took my last picture from the driver's seat just before I passed through the West Point gates. My burst of freedom was over.

The military yoke eases a bit for West Point firsties, but still I counted the days until graduation, unable to do anything except the bare minimum. I skated through classes and my military duties, but I strove to become a better climber with my whole heart. I climbed every chance I had. I traversed until I couldn't close my fingers on a stair railing. I ran, I lifted weights and did pull-ups in the gym after dark. At the slightest opportunity I sped to the Gunks in my truck.

It took a decade to live that last year at West Point. Cadets have a saying that perfectly describes the situation: "West Point is a hundred-and-fifty-thousand-dollar education shoved up your ass a nickel at a time." Only in recent years have I grown content with my attendance at West Point—it again feels unique, and perhaps a little adventurous. I'm glad I went, and I hope that the institution can one day find it in its stony heart to consider me a credit.

Since cadets don't pay for their education, they are obligated to serve in the active Army upon graduation. For four years I nursed the hope that life in the "real" Army would provide the meaningful experience that West Point did not. I opted into the infantry after graduation. I chose an assignment in a hard-charging light division at Fort Ord, California, and I attended Ranger School.

Ranger School is loaded with military mystique. It lasts fifty-eight days and nights and the students get an average of two and a half hours of sleep per night and one meal per day while they plan and execute arduous raid, ambush, and recon patrols designed to simulate wartime stress. All infantry officers are expected to "volunteer" for and graduate from Ranger School, and graduates of the school wear a black-and-gold shoulder tab on their uniforms. Any infantry officer who fails to earn the Ranger tab is branded a "tango foxtrot"—a tabless fuck—and is always considered with a raised eyebrow and regarded as if he has a missing leg. The first two weeks of the course were a constant stream of physical and mental torture designed to quickly wash out unmotivated candidates. People dropped in droves, and the attrition was fascinating to witness. One minute a guy would be soldiering along, apparently strong, and the next minute he'd quit, somehow unable to continue, and he would never be seen again. Day after day it rained and heavy pack straps cut into my shoulders as we lugged weapons toward some far-off objective. Ranger School is not an intellectual school; any physically fit soldier with common sense and heart can earn the tab, but all must suffer to get it. Hunger, exhaustion, and performance stress crushed out the niceties. Feelings were unimportant, totally subordinated to mission accomplishment. I like to think I did well at Ranger School, and my personal key came early in the course when I stopped dreading my next, inevitable dose of misery. I did not care about *anything* except getting that Ranger tab pinned onto my shoulder and onto the shoulders of my squad mates. Anything can be endured for fifty-eight days. Ranger School is as hard-core as the peacetime military gets, but it lacked the keen edge of adventure because the Ranger instructors are always there to supervise operational safety. Ranger School is hard, but it isn't like climbing in Patagonia. In Patagonia, there is no net.

I enjoyed much of my four years as an infantry platoon leader. To be totally responsible for the lives and welfare of a thirty-three-man platoon was *awesome,* and not in the slang sense. Much of an infantry-man's life is lived outdoors, and the challenges of intelligently ma-neuvering a tired, hungry, wet, and sleep-deprived platoon across unfamiliar ground at night were legion. But still, I never missed an opportunity to climb.

In the winter months I would finish work at five P.M. on a Friday, jump into my loaded truck, and drive nine hours from Monterey to Joshua Tree in the Mojave Desert, climb Saturday and Sunday, and drive nine hours home Sunday night to arrive in the battalion parking lot with just enough time to catch two hours of sleep before six A.M. formation for physical training on Monday morning. Happily, the granite walls of Yosemite were only four hours away for vertical for-ays during the warmer months. Once, in Yosemite, I caught a snippet of conversation in the Mountain Room Bar, after a day when most of us had been drenched by a surprise thunderstorm. "Yeah," quipped a veteran to his young partner, "but that was shit compared to being caught out in Patagonia." And so the hook set deeper.

We invaded Panama, but I got no closer to Patagonia than the northern edge of the Darien Gap, the stretch of jungle and swamp that separates Panama from Colombia. Patagonia still remained the length of a continent away, a distant dream. Back in the States I continued to build the breadth of my climbing experience despite my military obligations. I got over a major obstacle when I climbed Yosemite's El Capitan. I had been told that any aspirant to the great mountain ranges of the world needed to be comfortable on the big walls of Yosemite. Able I proved to be; comfortable I was not. Two days into the El Cap climb, we had 2,000 feet below us and the wall soared over our heads like a granite ocean. I couldn't even sense the top of the route a thou-sand feet above us. I was lost in a sea of vertical granite and awash in fear. Terrified, I dry-heaved off the edge of the ledge where we spent the night. My technical skills were good enough, but mentally I barely held it together, and for Patagonia I would need to be comfortable on walls of this magnitude.

The military has, at its base, the big stick. Behind every chewed ass is the UCMJ, the Uniform Code of Military Justice, and it is the real wellspring of the Army's order, the discipline of no other choice. There is no such alpine wellspring, for in the mountains, if you don't want to do it, you don't. Scratch the nonchalant attitude and playful grin of any serious climber, and you'll uncover the steel of patience and will. And the climber's is a real discipline, one that you can walk away from at any time without consequence but don't. An astonishing number of officers survive—hell, thrive and excel—on brash martial bluster backed up by hot air and bullshit, but the toughest people I know keep it to themselves. True toughness sits quietly, like the dull luster of a worn pair of combat boots or a battered ice axe. The culture of bluster and false dedication is found in the mountains as well, but it seldom reaches a summit, and it never gets promoted.

As much as anything, I think I revolted against the prescribed path, the horrifying security of a military career. Your peers and superiors constantly tell you what tick marks to make on the road to institutional success. To excel, the crucial thing is not to fail. Do what everyone else is doing, just do it a little better, and you're a stud. Do it a little worse, and you're a slug. You push the right buttons, leave a few people behind, the paycheck comes, you get promoted, punch the next layer of buttons, create the impression of hard work, get promoted, and so it goes until you retire.

One day on maneuvers at Fort Hunter-Liggett, my battalion commander, Tod J. Wilson, an officer I greatly respected, came around to inspect my antitank platoon. A week or so earlier I had tendered my resignation; I would leave active service in six weeks. A "lame duck" lieutenant, I was in a perfect position to call a spade a spade, a state of mind that Colonel Wilson actively encouraged. I had surprised no one when I'd handed in my resignation the morning after the post–Gulf War Army announced its new downsizing policy, designed to reduce the number of officers on active duty. The Army preferred to release those officers who wanted out rather than force out others.

Colonel Wilson concluded his inspection and we stood together in front of my Humvee and watched the afternoon shadows stretch across the dark purple and tarnished brass hills of central California.

"Crouch," he said, "I've been trying to go elk hunting with my dad for nineteen years. With the Army and all, I've never been able to make it happen. He's getting on now, and I don't know if we're ever going to do it." I considered his words and realized that my goal was not to be a high-ranking officer in charge of hundreds of men I barely knew. My military ambition had been to lead an infantry platoon, and I had done that—twice. To reach the mountains of my dreams I needed time, and time is one thing the Army doesn't often part with. Colonel Wilson and many others like him were and are up to the sacrifice, but I couldn't stomach the loss of my adult life.

My desire to make my own way left me with no draw toward corporate life. Squeezing time out of American business is even harder than squeezing it out of the Army. The money was better in the business world, but money wasn't the point. I've always wanted to build a wealth of experience, in life and in climbing, and no month of leave would ever suffice. I left the Army and took it on faith that by doing what I loved to do I would find enough to eat.

Now I can see that I learned tremendously from the Army. The Army took over where high school track and cross-country left off, and finished hammering out my basic shape. But I'm simply not an institutional man, and I resented its molding hands.

For my parents, my decision to leave the Army and go climbing was terrible. My father could no longer wear his West Point graduate and Army officer son like a medal among his cronies. My mom worried that I would lose any opportunity I might have had to find a career in the normal world. Both were worried that I'd die out there. My old man bombarded me with a semiannual stream of grad school applications, imagining my career as a broadcast journalist. He pressured me with every phone conversation. Each additional piece of news about the rising success of my West Point classmates—both in and out of the Army—was more difficult to bear. Everyone thought I was a bum. I lived in the margin, and it was increasingly hard to hold my mountain dreams.

I had a year's pay squirreled away when I left the Army, money that could have been a retirement nest egg or the down payment on a house, but it wasn't socked away with the vision of a doughnut-eating Greg lazing his way through his dotage with his feet up in front of a roaring fire. That money had a purpose, it was a tool, and it saw me across the years from the Army to the summit of Fitzroy.

•

After a winter of climbing rock in Hueco Tanks outside of El Paso and mountaineering in the high Andes of Ecuador, a long-standing relationship went in the tank, sunk by my cancerous restlessness and climbing fever. I wanted to move, she did not. In the aftermath I climbed like a man possessed. Pain substitution for sure, but my climbing ability jumped. I spent most of the next year living out of a VW bus, climbing in Colorado, Wyoming, and Yosemite Valley, where my second trip up El Cap was mental duck soup. When I left the Valley late that fall, I was in prime physical condition. Strong mentally and physically, I was ready for the step so long dreamed of. I sold the VW and swore that I'd never fix another one. I bought a plane ticket. I loaded a backpack. *"Alea jacta est,"* said Caesar as he sent his army across the Rubicon and irrevocably committed the Roman Republic to civil war. The die is cast. I went to Patagonia.

AN ANTIQUE TURNTABLE SCRATCHES OUT
tangos from the back of a bar in Cochrane, in Chilean Patagonia. My half-empty bottle of beer sweats a ring onto a wobbly table; the next should dull the pain caused by the hard
wooden seat. All the furniture in this place is handmade; the
floor is concrete. A film of grime clings to the lace curtains
that hang over the window. Outside, sheets of dust blow down
an unpaved street. The wind thrashes the trees in the town
square. Three strong, stout horses pass the bar for each battered pickup. A woman on her way to a backyard washtub just
hurried past the window carrying a black plastic trash bag
stuffed full of my dirty clothes. Since I've spent the better part
of a month in the mountains without a change of clothes, un-
told nastiness lurks in that bag.

Yesterday, we pulled back into Cochrane from our unsuccessful attempt to climb Cerro San Lorenzo, a colossus of
snow, ice, and rotten granite that straddles the Argentine frontier about forty miles to the southeast. Andrés Zegers, my
Chilean partner, stuck out his thumb and headed north a few

hours ago. I plan to rest here in Cochrane a day or two before I hitch-hike across into Argentina and on down to the Fitzroy massif. It has been a hard month.

•

Just after the New Year, my plane landed at a simple airport near Coihaique, 150 miles north of here. I filed down the stairs onto the tarmac and into the crucifying wind that swept the flight line. The other passengers braced and hustled to the terminal, but I just stood and stared across plains of thrashing grass to the hills beyond. The cool yellow light of late afternoon shimmered in waves on the tossing plains. Patagonia, at last Patagonia.

I linked up with Andrés in Coihaique. We'd met climbing in Yosemite back in September and October, and I stayed with his hospitable family in Santiago for two weeks on my way south. Andrés has straight brown hair that almost touches his shoulders, and he's strong and by far the most fanatic of all the Chilean climbers I have met. Also with him were Soames Floweree and Pablo Besser, two of his pals from Santiago. All of us planned to go to San Lorenzo together, but once there, Soames and Pablo planned to retrace the northern route of Padre Alberto María De Agostini, a Salesian brother and mountain explorer who made the first ascent of Cerro San Lorenzo in 1941. Andrés and I hoped to climb the mountain's East Ridge.

For two days the four of us hitchhiked from Coihaique to Cochrane down the Carreterra Austral—*the* road in southern Chile. We got rides in a VW bus, a logging truck, a cattle truck, a flatbed, and, finally, in the bed of a pickup. First we went through a landscape of rolling hills and long grass, then one of gnarled trees, roaring rivers, and emerald lakes backed by snow peaks and glaciers. Fierce wind dominated both geographies. The Carreterra Austral may be the great public work of Pinochet's military dictatorship, but the Santa Monica

Freeway it is not. It's not even paved. The second day only two cars passed us, both going in the other direction.

We were dropped off at the outskirts of Cochrane. A scruffy dog sniffed my heels. Chilean *pobladores* (pioneers) wearing riding gear and spurs stood in shadows and alcoves with their hats pulled down low. Horses stood patiently in front of the general store or gnawed at the grass in the town square. Trees bent under the weight of the wind. We hired a dented pickup to take us to the *confluencia* of the Río Tranquilo and the Río Salto.

The next day, we trudged up through foothills and spent the night a few miles short of the Argentine border. Soames and Pablo went up the last canyon before the frontier to find the base of the De Agostini Route. Andrés and I illegally crossed the border—San Lorenzo's East Ridge is in Argentina—and kept trudging around the mountain. The wind scudded an endless parade of clouds across the sky; rain squalls suddenly soaked everything. Above a tremendous glacier and a raging river, cascades of ice, slopes of snow, and buttresses of shattered granite rose into the churning cauldron. The summit of Cerro San Lorenzo, many thousands of feet above, remained hidden.

The sky blew clear during the last day that we sweated under our packs and scrambled over the exposed "dry" ice of the glacier toward the high pass formed between Cerro San Lorenzo's East Ridge and the unnamed crag to its east. I traced the immense line of the ridge with my eyes, not quite able to wrap my head around the scale of the Patagonian landscape. It seemed to take an hour of hard hiking to travel between the most minor features. But as improbably big as the landscape of Patagonia is, it is dwarfed by the sky that rides above it, a sky bigger than other skies, more wild, and so blue that it's almost black.

The long line of San Lorenzo's East Ridge dropped in a sweep from the summit into the pass, that pass an island of rock that divides the glacier on our side of the ridge from the one on the other. Among the rocks of the pass we hoped to find a site to locate our camp. We struggled up from the glacier into the pass, and thus began our days in base camp. In the nearly two weeks that we were based in that pass, we didn't see a single human trace—not a signpost, not a prepared tent site, not a bubble gum wrapper, not a footprint, not even so much as smoke from a far-off campfire. Our isolation was astonishing.

We cleared aside a patch of boulders, pitched the tent, and guyed it out to well-braced rocks. The clouds soon returned and the wind lashed sheets of rain against the tent; the rain turned to snow, and over four feet of it fell. We had to dig out the tent every few hours. The rest of the time I wrote in my journal or just lay there and followed my thoughts as they soared on the wings of the wind. It was one of the most adventurous experiences of my life, and I didn't go beyond a twenty-foot circle.

We could hear gusts roar into our ravine seconds before they shook the tent. I lived in fear of that one tremendous gust that would shred the tent and end our expedition in a chaotic frenzy of desperate retreat and unsheltered misery. I was torn off my feet by savage gusts—twice—while I was outside shoveling snow with our aluminum pot, and I was loath to imagine what would happen to a pair of alpinists caught high up on a peak by a storm that strong. It was a world of gray cloud, gray snow, and wind, broken once by the blinding light of the sun. In those moments before the clouds returned, we watched the wind tear an enormous snow banner from San Lorenzo's summit and scatter that snow like a streamer of glittering chiffon across the Patagonian sky. The raw natural power of this southern land plowed a furrow of fear through me.

Gradually, the snow building up around the tent protected us from the full effect of the wind. When the storm broke four days later the mountain wore a sheen of white snow and ice and looked like an enormous wedding cake. We packed our bags, ate, tightened our bootlaces, and went up. Even though San Lorenzo's summit elevation is a decidedly unimpressive 13,000 feet, its brute size should not be underestimated. San Lorenzo is massive, and I had never tried a mountain so big. We climbed simple snow slopes and over a long stretch of low-angle granite piled with dangerously loose blocks of stone. A decade of listening to stories detailing the savageness of Patagonian storms had made me deathly afraid of being caught out in one, and my fear mounted with every move. We climbed until last light, at about eleven P.M., and made a bivouac on a rocky perch from which— depending on the weather at dawn—we could continue up or easily get down.

Many times I peeked out into the night from the confines of my bivy sack. The towering ice walls of Cerro San Lorenzo and the glaciers that flow out from the mountain's feet gleamed dull silver under the light of a crescent moon.

Heavy flying-saucer clouds stood downwind of the peak as the sun rose. Ominous. We felt no wind, but I had heard that the Patagonian sky full of those flying-saucer clouds—lenticulars—is a classic harbinger of storm. I shivered in my thin bivy sack, full of doubt. The weather didn't look perfect. Should we press on, knowing we might get hammered high up on the peak, where it would be hard—perhaps impossible—to get down? Should we sit there and wait to see what the weather did? Or should we beat a hasty retreat and be certain of a clean escape? Which was the right course of action? I did not know.

We opted for retreat and were in camp by noon.

All the rest of that day, all the next night, and all of the following day I stared up at the pyramid peak of Cerro San Lorenzo and into a silent world of white, light, gray, stone, and ice with no wind and no storm. The weather held. We could have done it. The third day was also fine, but we didn't have the guts for another crack at San Lorenzo, so we nibbled at the toes of the giant by climbing Cerro Los Penitentes, one of the lesser peaks across from San Lorenzo—a summit, yes, but Cerro San Lorenzo was the prize, and he had crushed us with a mere threat.

The storm finally did return, but it didn't matter. We were broken; some days later we scraped the bottom of our food stash and began the long slog back to civilization. I felt San Lorenzo's stare on my back as we slithered away. Such a mountain relents only to a whole heart.

During the hike out, we stopped in at one of the *estancias* and were treated to a mutton stew, which, after so many days without any solid food, ranks as one of my life's great meals. Soames and Pablo had passed through on their way home a few days before. Andrés and I slept out front beside the vegetable garden, and we stayed on the next morning to help with a few chores while two young boys whooped around the yard with our helmets and ice axes. By a stroke of pure luck, the older brothers were taking down their season's load of wool by oxcart that day, so in keeping with the age-old infantry maxim of "Why walk when you can ride?" we did our last ten miles bumping along atop huge bags of shorn wool. Andrés and I didn't even get wet the three times that we forded the Río Tranquilo and the water rose high up the necks of the oxen. Those beasts are like tractors, slow but megastrong.

Midafternoon we arrived at the road head. The ranchers dropped their wool sacks next to a parked Toyota pickup and returned home, utterly unworried about their unattended wool. Andrés and I kicked back on the wool sacks and stared at the sky for six hours (there wasn't any other traffic) until a pair of geologists on a research project returned to their truck and took us the last twenty miles into Cochrane. And there, after showers, shaves, and a mountainous meal of steak, eggs, fries, and beer, we slept soundly in soft beds.

•

And so, seated among the spartan furnishings of this Cochrane bar, alone, with Andrés gone north and the barkeep not around, I tilt my chair back on its hind legs and prop my feet on an adjacent chair. I rest an elbow and forearm on the tabletop and hold the wet bottle of beer in my hand. A tango's lament scratches one side of my consciousness. Staring through the window into the dust and wind and the trees that thrash beyond, I raise the bottle to my lips, swallow cool bitter beer, and reflect on the recent expedition. Honesty in Patagonia hurts as much as it does at home, and the truth tastes like a mouthful of sour milk. We did not acquit ourselves well; I did not acquit myself well. New to Patagonia and afraid of this place, I kept myself one mental step removed from the action. I never pinned myself onto the leading edge of the ascent, and I never gave my absolute best in the instant it was demanded. I'll never conquer my fear—that task is beyond me— but I must learn to live alongside it. Only then will I be able to step into the action and wage ruthless alpine war. Only then, on the wings of my own confidence, will I ascend in Patagonia.

•

A condor flying straight between Cerro San Lorenzo and the peaks of the Fitzroy/Cerro Torre massifs would cover a distance of just over a hundred miles. If I could have figured out how to get my passport stamped I might well have just shouldered my load at the base of San Lorenzo's East Ridge and walked to Fitzroy. Walking would have been faster, cheaper, and much less hassle. Instead, it took me eight days and a thousand miles of walking, oxcarting, hitchhiking, and busing to go around three and a half sides of an enormous rectangle to cover those hundred miles.

From that Cochrane bar I hitchhiked alone to Chile Chico and across the border into Argentina. I traveled east through Los Antiguos and Perito Moreno to Caleta Olivia, an oil town on the Atlantic. In the desert south of Caleta Olivia I camped beside the ocean under a full moon at the edge of the desert. In the morning I thumbed down the coast to Río Gallegos, the biggest city in Argentine Patagonia. From Río G. I lucked into a ride on an out-of-service bus that took me inland and north across windy desert steppes to the town of El Calafate, where I spent a day gearing up for another mountain stint. The next day I bused four more hours across more desert steppes to finally arrive in Chaltén.

Drained from my recent labors before San Lorenzo, tired, and nursing a serious case of road blues, I fell in with three Argentine friends touring the natural wonders of Patagonia. The weather was abysmal—wind and intermittent rain—and we pitched our tents around a fire pit. With patience, smiles, and a slow pace we talked and laughed and kindled an enduring friendship. We slurped *mate* (a strong Paraguayan tea) through a steel straw, swilled red wine from tin cups, and slowly cooked choice cuts of beef and lamb over a bed of coals. I wolfed down meat by the kilo.

One afternoon I wandered into Chaltén to resupply us with meat and wine, drink a nice cup of coffee, and search for a climbing partner. In the four days that I have been camped outside Chaltén I have not yet even seen Cerro Fitzroy, but I am not ignorant of its history, and another climber in the café pointed out to me that the man getting up from the corner table was none other than José Luis Fonrouge. I popped to my feet, tipped my chair over, and stumbled over it as I rushed across the café to shake his hand. Tall, thin, still in fine shape, and wearing a fleece sweater, Fonrouge looked to be about fifty, and he is one of my ultimate alpine heroes. Fonrouge isn't one of the twentieth century's most well known climbers, but the climb that he and his partner, Carlos Comesaña, pulled off on Fitzroy in January 1965 stands to me as one of the ultimate examples of a good ascent.

·

Midnight between the fourteenth and fifteenth of January 1965, and the dark Patagonian sky was quiet.

Cerro Fitzroy, that massive wedge of malevolent Patagonian granite, soared above two hammocks suspended inside a crevasse. Nestled inside were two hotshot Argentine climbers—Fonrouge and Comesaña—and they tried to sleep through the silence. The stars shimmered in a sea of black velvet. Fitzroy had been climbed only once, twelve years before, and from the opposite side. Both climbers had their hopes pinned on the weather. Forty-eight hours of good weather would give them a chance, a fair chance. The immense couloir that split the mountain above their heads already had a name, La Super-canaleta, the Supercouloir, even though it had never been climbed. The Supercouloir is an enormous natural line, a 6,000-foot gash in the west-northwest aspect of Fitzroy that faces directly into the teeth of the worst weather in the world.

Carlos Comesaña was twenty-three, José Luis Fonrouge three years younger. But despite their youth, they had lots of Patagonian experience between them. At fifteen, Fonrouge had made the second ascent of the Torre Norte in the Torres del Paine, another region of spectacular granite peaks a hundred miles to the southwest. Two years later he made an alpine-style attempt on Fitzroy's West Face, an undertaking so far ahead of its time that it wasn't actually done until the last month of the century. Climbs in France and intense training on the rocks of Cerro Catedral outside of Bariloche, which Fonrouge called their "laboratory," rounded out their experience. For seven years their whole lives had been focused on training for Fitzroy. A few days earlier the team made the first ascent of Guillaumet, one of Fitzroy's satellite peaks, a climb they considered a warm-up. Fonrouge and Comesaña were aflame with desire to climb Fitzroy.

At first light, the Argentines shouldered their gear. Their rack of hardware consisted of sixteen pitons, two wooden wedges for wide-crack protection, an ice screw, slings, and carabiners—a very light selection. Two hundred and fifty feet of bicolored rope, crampons, a piton hammer and an ice axe each, two down sleeping bags, hammocks, a gas stove, and three days of food completed their loads. They had the bare minimum, nothing more. This project would be no siege by a huge, well-supported team. No lifeline of fixed rope would secure their retreat to safe ground. Fonrouge and Comesaña planned a rapid climb and descent, depending on speed and skill to thread an ascent into this gap between storms.

Fonrouge and Comesaña's crampons bit into the hard frozen snow that led up into the massive couloir. The silence was pregnant, fractured only by the pick and kick of ice axes and crampons, their echoing voices, and the occasional clatter and whir of falling stones.

They moved together up the forty-five- to fifty-degree, 3,000-foot-long tongue of ice that rose into the couloir, making good time up this easy ground. High up the ice, the couloir split into two parallel bands divided by a ridge of granite. Just above the split Fonrouge and Comesaña moved onto rock. Visually satisfied that the route above was only rock, they stashed their crampons to trim weight. The Argentines struggled up chimneys, steep rock, and the odd overhang to the base of an enormous stone amphitheater formed by the sweep of rock that wraps left across the top of the couloir from Fitzroy's West Ridge.

At sundown they strung the hammocks, removed their boots, and struggled into their light sleeping bags. More than half of the vertical distance to the summit lay below, but 2,000 feet of climbing still stood between them and Fitzroy's summit. The sudden arrival of a storm would wreck their hopes.

Their preparation had been careful, detailed, and prolific; their motivation was extreme. Fonrouge considered the state of his and Comesaña's physical condition in 1965 to have been *inmejorable* ("unimprovable"). All depended on the capricious Patagonian weather— would it hold for one more day?

At dawn the Argentines were on the move again. Every pitch was a discovery, for no human had ever touched this stone. The rising path of least resistance led the team up and right across the huge amphitheater toward the West Ridge. The climbing was difficult, on a par with the hardest yet done in the European Alps, a much more benign range. After about fifteen rope lengths they gained the crest of the ridge and got a view of the three magnificent towers across the valley—Cerro Torre, Torre Egger, and Cerro Standhardt.

They took no extra time to devour the view, but pressed on up the ridge and wound their way around towers of rock brushed with ice. A wild view down the entire Supercouloir lurked below the last traverse to the summit slopes. Comesaña shared a few handfuls of peanuts and candy with his partner. The sun plunged toward the horizon, but only an hour separated Fonrouge and Comesaña from the consummation of their dream. They climbed on, up to the narrow summit of Fitzroy, the second party to share that triumph. Tears filled their eyes. Low in the western sky, the sun reflected a brilliant yellow off the Southern Patagonian Ice Cap.

The summit was calm, dead calm, but a line of clouds gathering far to the west showed that the stable weather would soon end. After an hour on top, they replaced the carabiner left on the summit by the great French alpinists Lionel Terray and Guido Magnone, the only others to visit Fitzroy's summit, with a small Argentine flag and descended into the evening.

By one A.M. they were a thousand feet down, at the top of the big amphitheater, but now a storm had its teeth into them. The lord of Patagonia, briefly negligent, was now violently awake. They spent their second night dangling from the walls of Fitzroy thrashed by wind. The storm hurled every weapon at the pair—wind, snow, cold, and slinging ice. The descent the next day was a desperate fight for survival. Wind and cloud howled around the rappelling climbers. They had to rig anchors to secure each of their rappels. One by one they left all their pitons and slings, their one ice screw, and even their hammer cords. The storm careened between the granite walls that enclose the Supercouloir. The rope became half-frozen; it was difficult to pull after each rappel. As they pulled one rappel, the wind blew the falling rope into a tangle in the rock above and to the side. They couldn't reach the tangle and had to cut the rope in order to continue their descent with the part of the rope they still controlled. Time and again the rope got stuck, and time and again they had to cut it. With only sixty-five feet of cord left, Fonrouge and Comesaña independently climbed down the final thousand feet to the glacier. There, the exhausted Argentines tied into their fragment of rope and fled across the crevassed glacier to the safety of base camp.

Fonrouge's and Comesaña's climb of the Supercouloir is the best first ascent ever made in Patagonia. They rose to meet the mountain on its own terms and employed only the purest tactics and left us a demanding legacy: a team of two blasting up an immense unclimbed line in uncompromised alpine style. The Supercouloir's first ascent sets the bar that all of us who climb in Patagonia should strive to live up to.

The storm that chased the successful pair from the slopes of Fitzroy raged for forty-five days.

•

Buzzed with coffee and from having shaken the hand of one of my heroes, I tote a bag of mutton, *mate,* and four liters of red wine back
down the road to our tent site. The weather is still awful, blown rain
pelts my jacket, and I haven't yet caught a single glimpse of the mountains that are supposed to stand behind the foothills. I have no fixed
climbing objective. Hell, I don't even have a partner, but I'd at least
like to try to climb something. There is one alpine weapon that I do
possess in abundance, however, and that is time. It's now the last day of
January, and my flight home from La Paz, Bolivia, isn't until the end of
July. I've got time, and that's a good thing, because the geography and
climate of the Southern Hemisphere conspire to stack the Patagonian
deck heavily against the aspirations of a climber nursing a tight schedule.

Only 30 percent of the surface of the globe is dry land, and most
of that land lies in the Northern Hemisphere. And in the Southern
Hemisphere, with the obvious exception of Antarctica, most of the
land is found above 30° south latitude. Between 30° south and the
shores of Antarctica at about 70° south, the world's surface is almost
entirely water. The only significant land masses between 30° and 40°
south are the Cape of Good Hope at the bottom of Africa, the southern slice of Australia, and the North Island of New Zealand. Below 40°
there is just Tasmania, the South Island of New Zealand, and the long
southern finger of South America—Patagonia. Sure, other islands dot
this great southern sea, but they are only pinpricks, and this enormous
cold ocean rules the climate of Patagonia. In order to understand why,
one must examine the general global weather patterns.

Ten degrees to either side of the equator is the region that sailors
call the doldrums, a belt of fickle winds and active thunderstorms that
are fed by the northeast trade winds from the north and the southeast
trades from the south. As the northeast and southeast trades converge,

the atmosphere has nothing to do but rise, and rise it does, causing a semipermanent belt of low pressure around the equator. The rising air flows out to the north and south and subsides in the subtropics at about 30° north and south latitudes. This sinking air causes belts of high pressure called the subtropical highs to exist at the northern and southern edges of the tropics. Moving away from the equator in both directions, from about 30° to 60° of latitude (the mid-latitudes) is an active belt of prevailing westerly winds. Poleward from the westerlies is a zone of generally low pressure that rings both poles at about 60°. These two "circumpolar troughs" are where the storm fronts that swarm across the mid-latitudes go to die. In the Northern Hemisphere, the landmasses of Eurasia and North America break up the circumpolar trough into two storm cemeteries—the Aleutian Low in the North Pacific and the Icelandic Low at the top of the Atlantic. South, however, in the circumpolar trough that rings Antarctica, there are no such continental obstacles, and 60° south is the only place where a line of latitude runs all the way around the globe without hitting dry land.

The fact that the ocean can flow freely around the globe at 60° south keeps the ocean of the high southern latitudes cold. The continental dams of Eurasia and North America allow ocean currents like the Gulf Stream and the Japan Current to rush warm tropical waters far north in the Northern Hemisphere. These warm currents help keep the average annual temperature of the Northern Hemisphere one degree Celsius warmer than the Southern Hemisphere. No such warm currents disturb the cold ocean temperatures of the high southern latitudes, and climatically speaking, that one degree makes an immense difference.

In both hemispheres, air wants to move from the subtropical high pressures at 30° toward the circumpolar low pressures at 60°. This air gets a strong kick from the Coriolis effect as it moves—a kick to the left in the Southern Hemisphere and a push to the right in the Northern. So pressure forces acting in concert with the Coriolis effect spawn the prevailing westerlies of the mid-latitudes. The larger the temperature difference between 30° and 60°, the stronger the pressure forces will be and the stronger the corresponding winds, and since the temperature difference between 30° and 60° tends to be larger in the Southern Hemisphere, that is where the strongest west winds blow.

The overall weather picture is simpler and more regular in the Southern Hemisphere, because there aren't such huge landmasses to jolt the system. Cold and warm fronts form in the Southern Hemisphere, usually between 30° and 40° south latitude, when warm tropical air collides with cooler mid-latitude air, but because there isn't much land to cause large contrasts of temperature and moisture, the fronts themselves aren't as strong as they are in the north. What start as cold and warm fronts in the Southern Hemisphere quickly lose their individual characteristics and adopt the character of the ocean beneath: cold and wet. These broad storm bands of cool, moist air swept along by the west wind migrate to the east-southeast as they are gradually sucked toward the circumpolar trough around Antarctica. But the circumpolar trough isn't always the same; it waxes and wanes. It's prone to wax large and stay large and lap over the southern end of the Americas. When it does, the atmospheric pressure in Patagonia goes down and stays down, a succession of wet storms are sucked over the Andes, and the vile weather in the mountains can last for weeks.

The Patagonian Andes act like a ramp and the air suddenly rises. The abrupt rise further cools the air and condenses its moisture into cloud, cold rain, or snow, and with the passing aeons that precipitation has formed the glaciers and ice caps of the Patagonian Andes. And the air can actually accelerate as it plunges down again after its rise up the hump of the Andes, a downslope effect similar to the Alps' foehn and the Rockies' chinook, downslope effects that magnify the power of wind.

Good weather does happen in Patagonia; it just doesn't happen very often. When rare clear and windless conditions do prevail, they're usually caused by a "blocking anticyclone" or a "blocking high," so called because they block the normal west-to-east migration of the storms. When the jet stream of fast-moving winds that circles the globe at high altitudes above the mid-latitudes splits into two branches, one jet goes far north and the other goes far south, and a high-pressure system forms in the fork. This is the blocking high, and it usually has an accompanying "cutoff low" to the north, so the whole weather setup puts the cutoff low in place of the normal high pressure at 30° south and the blocking high in place of the normal low at about 50° south. One half of the jet stream goes north around the high, the other branch goes far to the south, and both branches miss Patagonia. Since the jet stream steers the west winds, and the west winds drive the storms, when the jet stream is diverted no storms assault Patagonia.

A blocking anticyclone isn't stable for the long run, and it gradually erodes, but a strong blocker and the good weather under it can last three or four days, sometimes even up to a week. Stories of perfect weather that lasts twenty days and more pepper Patagonian lore, but I've never seen anything close. The best it has ever done for me is eight days of more or less nice weather, but even that megaspell was split in half by a storm that lasted thirty hours.

Consider it a legitimate Patagonian good spell if the pause between storms lasts forty-eight hours, but clear, windless Patagonian skies often last only thirty hours, and even more often such fine conditions don't last eighteen hours. The worst kind of "good spell" is the thirty-hour variety, as it lasts just long enough for an alpinist to climb high up a peak and get caught there by the next storm. But a line is crossed somewhere between thirty and forty-eight hours of good weather, and as Patagonian hotshot Rolando Garibotti says, "If you get forty-eight hours of good weather and don't get it done, you don't deserve it."

•

Four days of meat, wine, and fine company have recharged my alpine batteries, and in the morning I break camp, load my backpack, and labor uphill toward the Río Blanco base camp. Step by slow step I trudge up a long, forested hill and then more easily over flat terrain toward forests and the next foothills. A storm churns across the sky, and the brown-yellow bases of the granite satellites of Fitzroy are like tree trunks beneath the cloud layer. Mists whirl around the stone buttresses. Gray-white glaciers flow down toward me from the feet of the peaks. Sweat and occasional rain trickle down my forehead. I slog along and the clouds rise and peel apart and reveal the full open horseshoe sweep of Fitzroy and his satellites. I flop down beside the track and lean against my pack. Fitzroy, that huge, enormous, immense wedge, stands against the gray sky at the back of the horseshoe, smaller alpine needles spread out to either side. I'm still many miles from its base, but Fitzroy seems planted in my face. It's twice as big as I expected, and I expected very big. Fitzroy is the best mountain I have ever seen in my life.

I sit there for five minutes, my vision of alpine perfection met and exceeded. Mountains so impossibly good demand action. I struggle to my feet and make haste for base camp.

I teeter across the Río Blanco on a bridge of fallen logs and climb up the far bank into the beech forest. A few yards beyond is the climbers' base camp. It is a dank, dreary place. Little sun ever penetrates the foliage, and the forest floor is black and boggy. There is no view of the peaks. Crude log huts house climbers from many expeditions. I poke my head into the first with an introductory smile and am rebuffed by "This is a German-speaking hut." At the next, "This is a French-speaking hut" sends me packing. I discover my tribe in the scruffiest, most uncomfortable, and most dilapidated hut at the back of camp. Pablo—my recent companion on the Carreterra Austral hitchhike and the San Lorenzo approach—greets me with a bear hug and introduces his partner Waldo Farias, also of Santiago. Pablo, cut from passionate Latin cloth, joins me in a Spanish and English rant against the mothers of the elitist Euros in the cush huts. I fall in easily with him and the other linguistic exiles. There's Miyazaki Motohiko from Japan, two Slovenians, two Argentines, and Steve Schraeder and Forrest Murphy from Washington State. All are my kind of happy dirtbags.

Pablo and Waldo let me toss my lot in with theirs. The weather cracks and we make a move toward Fitzroy. We hope to climb the Franco-Argentine Route, which rises from La Brecha de los Italianos, the high col between Fitzroy and Poincenot first reached by an Italian team that attempted Fitzroy unsuccessfully in 1937. In late 1951 a French team led by Lionel Terray came south to take a crack at Fitz. Terray was one of the world's best climbers. He had made dozens of important ascents in the Alps, including the second ascent of the Eiger's North Face, and was a key member of the team that made the first ascent of Annapurna in 1950, the first of the world's 8,000-meter peaks to be climbed. Juan and Evita Perón wined and dined the Frenchmen in Buenos Aires and lent their support and prestige to the enterprise. At the behest of the dictator, the Argentine army trucked the expedition to the end of the road in Patagonia.

There were no bridges across the Río de las Vueltas or the Río Fitzroy in the early fifties, and one member of the team, Jacques Poincenot, drowned while crossing the Río Fitzroy. The Frenchmen christened the alpine steeple immediately left of Fitzroy Aguja Poincenot and elected not to abandon their expedition. Five weeks later, after epic battles with the weather, Terray and Guido Magnone were in a well-stocked snow cave dug into La Silla (a seat of snow on the south flank of Fitzroy just right of La Brecha). The Frenchmen held out in the cave until the weather turned good. Terray and Magnone climbed straight up for a few hundred feet and then followed the circuitous path of least resistance that wandered out right, then up, and then way back left to the summit snow slopes. Their route looks like a sideways horseshoe. They spent two nights on the mountain, and the good weather held just long enough for them to reach the summit and leave the carabiner that Fonrouge and Comesaña would find twelve years later when they topped out the Supercouloir.

In the 1970s alpinists began repeating routes on Fitzroy, and both the Supercouloir and the California Route (established by Yvon Chouinard and four friends, a group known as the Funhogs) saw multiple repeats. The French Route never became popular because of its circuitous nature. Climbers like to go straight up.

In 1984, an Argentine team returned to the section of Fitzroy's southeast face above La Silla that the French had climbed. They followed the original line up for a few hundred feet, but where Terray and Magnone had semicircled way out right, up, and back left, the Argentines blasted straight up a steep series of beautiful dihedrals that cut out the wandering of the French Route. The Argentines rejoined the French line a few rope lengths below the summit snows, and their variation on the original French climb is called the Franco-Argentine Route. The climbing is good on solid rock, and it is not too desperately hard to get down the route in a storm because the crux corners of the Argentine variation are protected from the worst of the wind. It is by far the most frequently attempted route up Fitzroy.

The exact line of the Terray-Magnone route up Fitzroy has never been repeated.

The sun is fierce and sweat soaks our long underwear and runs off our heads as we wade through the new snow that lies knee deep on the glaciers and snowfields that lead to Paso Superior. The pass gives access to the headwaters of the Piedras Blancas Glacier, the glacier that drains the east side of Fitzroy. On the glacier the fresh stuff is thigh deep. We take turns breaking trail.

We climb 1,000 feet of snow, ice, and rock to La Brecha. It's almost night, so we spread our sleeping gear on a flat perch, cook, and settle in for the night. We oversleep and it's light by the time we finally get moving.

Two Austrians race past us on their way to the summit of Fitzroy. We are moving, but not at the speed of a lightning alpine raid. We plod, burdened by too much equipment and inefficient systems, and use most of the day to get over the dihedrals of the Argentine variation. At the top of the dihedrals I lead the pitch up and left from the southeast to the southwest side of a steep buttress to the point where we rejoin the original French Route. From the top of that pitch the view goes west over a deep valley to the Torres on the far side and the ice cap beyond. Out there, dark clouds like berets top dozens of summits. A storm is coming. Waldo and Pablo want to press on, but I don't have the guts to drive on for the summit and almost surely get caught high up. We back off a few hundred feet to a ledge and spend the night. If the weather holds good we'll go up in the morning. The only vindication for my lack of fortitude is that the storm does hit in the morning. It's a little one, at most a Patagonian C–, but it'd be much worse higher, and the ministorm does dish out my first taste of Patagonian foul weather retreat. That taste notches up my confidence, and I need it, since the only way I'm going to handle the fear of a full-bore alpine blitzkrieg is to have confidence in my ability to escape back down.

We flee to base camp.

All along, my story in base camp has been that although I'd love to climb something—Fitzroy would be my first choice—I'm just in Patagonia this first time to check things out, see what the deal is, to get the feel of the place, and if I get lucky and get on top of a peak, so much the better. But inwardly, ever since that first view of Fitz and especially since the recent failure with Pablo and Waldo, the story I tell myself is quite different. Privately, I am consumed with ambition. Alone in my tent and tucked into my sleeping bag, I ball my fist and bang it off the nylon floor. "Goddamnit," I mutter, "you blew *another* opportunity. Those Austrians proved it was a good one." Some Patagonian seasons provide only one; I hope that I have not squandered the only one allotted to me. I want so badly to stand on top of Fitzroy that it knots my stomach. I so badly want to be good enough. I can hardly sleep.

•

The hut is crowded because it's breakfast time and it's raining. The A-frame hut is long and skinny and a split log suspended by ropes from the ceiling runs down the middle as a kind of swinging table. We cook in shifts, rotating to the two spots farthest from the door, where a raised platform provides an irregular cooking surface. Forrest and I scootch to the far end. He fries a pan of eggs and potatoes for himself and Steve, and I boil water for hot chocolate. Somewhere in my travels one of my stove's wire pot supports fell off unnoticed, so my stove has only three supports instead of four. The stove works fine, but it's hard to balance the pot that sits on top. My water is at a roiling boil and I clutch it with my pot grips, but I don't get a clean grip on the rim and the pot slips. It hits the wire supports and since the one is missing it tips over, and a quart of boiling water spills straight onto Forrest's foot. He's wearing only socks and sandals.

We stand outside in the rain. Forrest's face is contorted in pain and he has his scalded foot sunk into a trickle of water that runs past our hut. I look down at Forrest's red and swollen foot and I know for a fact that he is not going to be able to put that foot in a mountain boot or a climbing shoe for weeks. Forrest knows it too, and although his words reassure me that it was just an accident, his eyes tell me that I'm the most careless asshole he has ever seen and that he'd like to yank my heart out on the pick of an ice axe. I can't begrudge him such sentiment. I lost my concentration for a second, and I ruined his trip. I wish it were my foot, and I feel like a turd, but that doesn't stop me from snagging his now-available partner, Steve, for another attempt on Fitzroy.

The weather doesn't look great the next day, but the wind isn't blowing and I am determined to make another attempt—a better attempt. We're about to leave camp late in the afternoon when Boris Strmšek, one of the Slovenians, asks to join us. He and his partner have been trying to climb Fitzroy for five weeks and his partner doesn't have the motivation for another go. Boris asks to join us, he practically begs to join us, and I, who up until yesterday was in exactly the same partnerless boat, can't say no. Besides, Forrest's foot was a huge hit to my mountain karma, and it needs maintenance. Boris runs off to stuff his pack. A quarter of an hour later we go up.

•

For the next twenty-one hours, Boris, Steve, and I put everything we have into climbing this monstrous wedge of snow and ice-plastered stone. It's not enough. We're under attack from a clear-sky storm. Demonic Patagonian wind screams in from the west. Gusts are visible to the naked eye from miles away. Ice crystals borne by the ferocious wind make the gusts shimmer as they rage toward our perch high on the slopes of Cerro Fitzroy. Six hundred impossible feet separate us from Fitzroy's summit.

There isn't a storm cloud in the sky, but a high layer of gray obscures the blue above. Views stretch for miles across the splendor of the Patagonian Andes, but the wind tries to tear out our souls. We've trespassed into a forbidden realm.

All last night and all day today we climbed, slowed by a paper-thin sheen of verglass ice that covered all exposed granite. Ice choked every crack. The layer of cloud blocked the sun's rays all day and the ice never melted. Every single hold had to be hacked free of ice. Blood now oozes from a dozen wounds on my hands. In the late afternoon, we neared Fitzroy's shoulder and easier climbing. Then the wind started to rise . . .

At first gentle breezes caressed our clothing, then more insistent forces tugged at us. An hour later, and we are engulfed in swirling madness. This wind is the apocalypse unleashed. No clouds march in from the west to add tangible presence to our desperate situation, but unseen demons attack us from all sides—updrafts, downdrafts, and side blasts. The only clues to the gusts' approach are the shimmering ice crystals driven before the malevolent winds. We make one more defiant rope length of progress in the maelstrom, then abandon ascent. The summit of Fitzroy might as well be on Mars for all the hope we have of reaching it.

The irresistible, furious, driving, screaming, howling wind destroys my frame of reference. Nothing in my decade of climbing experience has prepared me for this preternatural anger.

Like fools we throw the ropes down the rock face as we prepare to rappel—only to see them rejected and blown back at us by a terrible updraft. I fight down on rappel first, and soon I'm out of sight of Boris and Steve. The free ends of the ropes thrash around like a pair of crazed bullwhips. I hope to arrive at a ledge I see below. I rappel past an over-hang and, swinging in space, I realize that the ends of the rope aren't going to reach the ledge. They don't even come close.

I've got a death grip with both hands on my rappel ropes. There are no knots in the ends of the ropes, and if I rappel off the ends of these ropes I am going to take a very long, very fatal fall down the southern side of Fitzroy.

I dangle in space below the overhang. Horrendous gusts grab me and batter me against the granite and spin me around in crazy cir-cles. My world degenerates into a chaotic swirl of sky, stone, and wind—Aguja Poincenot–sky–Cerro Torre–stone-SLAM-sky–Aguja Poincenot–sky–Cerro Torre–stone-SLAM—I spin around like a top. Fear clamps my guts.

Great rushes of wind careen around the peak with sharp gunfire cracks. The storm sounds like a locomotive as it drives through the high pass between Aguja Poincenot and Fitzroy. Furious gusts buffet me. "Do something, you damned fool," I tell myself. "You can't just swing around like a side of beef."

I can barely brush the tips of my toes against the stone below the overhang. It's not enough purchase to help. I focus and wrap the ropes around one of my thighs and tie a knot in the slack below my leg as the wind body-slams me into immovable stone.

I feel better with a knot tied—now I can't slide off the ends of the ropes—and I concentrate on solving my problem. I must get back up the ropes to a point above the overhang and set up an anchor. I try to ignore the invisible storm that claws at my every effort while I rig a friction knot with a spare sling to grip the ropes above my belay plate. I spin, twist, swing, and bounce—to my utter amazement I realize that updrafts are actually lifting my entire body weight. I hitch two slings to the friction knot and stand a foot into this improvised stirrup. I stand in the stirrup and cinch the belay plate at my waist up six inches, then slide the friction knot–stirrup combination six inches higher. Again and again I repeat the process, pummeled and twisted by the wind.

An age passes as I inch my way up to the overhang. Boris and Steve can't see me and communication in this wind is so obviously impossible that I don't bother to yell.

I reach the lip of the overhang with my friction knot–belay plate raising system. My concentration is so complete that I haven't noticed Steve is on rappel on the same ropes as I am—directly above the overhang. Our eyes meet. Steve's eyes widen to circles to show his surprise at still finding me on the ropes.

Somehow Boris and Steve had managed to pull up some slack and set up Steve's rappel. Then Steve had descended, all the while without realizing that my full weight still hung on the ropes. Without the help of the wind it would take the lifting power of a crane to pull slack into a rappel rope with a person dangling his full weight onto the other end. No human can do it—no pair of humans can do it.

Finally I am above the overhang. Steve, on the ropes above me, spots a rock horn and slings it for an anchor. As soon as the storm will allow we are off rappel and Boris joins us. Steve and I don't try to understand how the two of us ended up on the same rappel ropes. With a few more rappels we can make the shelter of a corner system facing east that ought to be out of the worst of this wind. Escaping the grasp of these demons of air is our sole thought—and our only hope of survival. The three of us get set to retrieve the rappel . . . only to discover the ropes won't pull.

All three of us pulling can't budge the ropes. What has gone wrong? The wind tries to tear the ropes from our grasp. It takes all our strength just to hang on as the ropes arc away in the hellish wind. I grab a pair of ascenders and prepare to climb the stuck ropes. Doing nothing is not an option.

I clamp my ascenders to one of the ropes and apply my full weight. "They're slipping!" I yell, and relief floods me.

Steve collects the loose end of the pulling rope to stop it from flying about in the wind. I bounce my full weight up and down and labor the ropes down inch by inch.

Suddenly, the balance of forces changes.

The wind rips the ropes loose through the anchor above, and flings them wildly across the face of Fitzroy. We reel in the loose rope in a panic, praying the rope won't snag on a flake or in a crack. Moments later we have both ropes under control at our position. Boris, in his broken English, suggests at the top of his lungs that we make shorter, more controllable rappels with just one rope.

Boris leads us down a few short rappels. Darkness falls as we fight to establish an anchor above the crucial corner system we hope will protect us from the ravages of the wind. Then, guided by the glow of my headlamp, I lower myself to a small ledge at the top of the corners and discover myself sheltered from the worst assaults. The wind screams through the darkness, but the fiercest gusts can't quite touch me. Boris and Steve come down to my stance. Denied their quarry, the wind demons howl ceaselessly, but we are finally beyond their reach. We breathe a collective sigh of relief, take stock of our situation, and continue down into blackness.

It takes all night to descend the several thousand feet to the glacier below the East Face of Fitzroy and a couple more hours to get from there down to base camp. We split up in camp, eat, and collapse into our tents. We haven't slept in two nights.

I get up, eat dinner, then sleep all night. Boris has to go home, and in the morning I carry a load of gear down to Chaltén to help speed him on his way. His bus is due to leave the next afternoon. We exchange good-byes and I return to camp. Steve and Forrest are also leaving in the hopes that by the time they get to Bariloche, Forrest's foot will be able to stand some lower-intensity rock climbing on the crags of Cerro Catedral.

That night, I again sleep like a dead man.

The barometric pressure rises steadily overnight. The clouds begin to part at ten A.M., and one of the Argentine climbers tells me that the pressure is the highest it has been in seven weeks. An electric current runs through base camp as everyone prepares their equipment. Everyone except me, that is. With Boris and Steve gone I don't have a partner, and I can only watch the others organize their sorties. I am beside myself: I can't read, I can't sleep, and I can't sit in my tent and do nothing. By noon the sky is clear and windless, and by two o'clock parties begin to go up to Paso Superior, where they'll eat a meal, kick out their sleeping bags, and sleep until midnight. By four P.M. camp is deserted. As each minute creeps past, another piece of my Patagonian dream seeps into the blue sky.

•

"Greg! Greg! Are you here?" I jump up to find the voice. I dodge through the trees and see Boris with a pack on his back and sweat pouring down his face and a big, big smile on his face. The smile on his face says "let's climb." The smile on mine says "hell, yes."

"I have food," he says in his thick Slovenian accent. "Let's eat, then go up."

Boris pulls a loaf of bread and a thick wad of beef from among the essentials in his pack. I kindle a fire with a splash of white gas and stuff my pack while a half-dozen small steaks sizzle over the flames. I lace my boots. Boris and I pass water bottles back and forth, slugging big gulps in preparation for the coming action. I am through the roof. Boris isn't as outwardly ebullient, but the fact that he has already covered six mostly uphill miles from town at a half run speaks volumes. He has decided to skip his bus and miss his plane for this one last chance to climb Fitzroy. I chomp one steak sandwich, then another. To save weight we're not going to take a stove up Fitzroy. We will have nothing but peanuts and chocolate bars until the push is over, so I pack down a third sandwich and take a last sip of water. A rush of cold sweat wets my face and scalp. I ate too much. My gut bucks and clutches, acid in my throat. I double over and vomit. A thick stream of puke splashes off the forest floor onto my boots. I hurl again; there goes the last of the water and good chow I had socked away. Back and stomach pain almost drive me to my knees.

"Aaah . . . fuck . . ." I hack my throat clear. My middle convulses and I double over again. This time it's dry. Tears stream down both my cheeks. I straighten up and look over at Boris. His eyes are wide like carabiners.

"I'm all right, I'm all right . . ." I snuffle and wipe my eyes dry with the back of a wrist. "Let's go." We step carefully around the vomit puddle, hoist our packs, and head uphill. By the time we get out of camp it's almost nine P.M.

•

Less than an hour above base camp we skirt the shores of Laguna de los Tres with the last light of day. We put on our headlamps and climb a glacier, scramble up a few rock steps, and then trudge up a series of snowfields toward Paso Superior. The half-dozen parties in front of us have left a well-broken trail through the snow and the going is easy. Our loads are light: no bivy gear, no stove or cook kit, two liters of water, and a double handful of food. I've even left my camera behind to save weight. I trust that Boris, who is a professional photographer, will take plenty of photos. I don't care about the memory of this climb. I just want to do the damned thing.

Right at midnight we trudge into Paso Superior. The others are stirring and cooking but we don't stop to do anything except grab my ropes and hardware out of doubled-up garbage bags and say hello and good luck as we head out the far side of the pass onto the Piedras Blancas Glacier. An hour or two later we flake the rope out below the bergschrund at the top of the glacier and watch the headlamps of the others bob up our tracks toward us. Above is the familiar thousand feet of snow and ice broken by a few sections of stone that lead up to La Brecha. We go up, we go up well, and few words are necessary. A few hours later we pop over La Brecha, descend a few meters on the far side, and turn right toward La Silla and the steep stone wall of Fitzroy's southeastern flank. By dawn we are one rope length up the stone. A few hundred feet higher I jam my hands into the coarse crux cracks of the Argentine variation, dodge a few patches of ice, and go up. The climbing is wonderful; the views are better. I feel as if I have grown wings.

This is our chance and we both know it. We are two men possessed. We have few common words and can hold no complicated conversations. Most humor is out of the question. But we do have a common obsession—both of us are willing to do whatever it takes to get to the top of Fitzroy. I've thrown the switch that I first touched as a runner in high school and learned well at Ranger School: This is the third night in five that I have gone without sleep but I don't care. I am hungry but I don't care. I am thirsty but I don't care. My hands are cut and swollen and it hurts to use them, but I don't care. I've never been so strong before in my life. Not one thing divides me from the action. All I care about is going up.

Higher up we make an error of route selection. Instead of traversing left we decide to go straight up. The low-angled summit slopes are farther away than they look and the decision costs us a few hours, but the mistake doesn't break our morale. Boris climbs a steep icy bulge and reaches the summit slopes. Boris leads these easy ice slopes, and I have a hell of a hard time coming up second because I left my crampons at the top of La Silla in an ill-advised plan to save weight. Without my crampons' metal spikes on my boots I slip and slide and pitch over sideways on the wind-polished thirty-degree ice. Finally the ice ends and we scramble over easy rocks to the very top.

I look around and am stunned to discover myself on the summit of Fitzroy. Boris and I grin, shake hands, and bear hug. I look around and try to soak up every detail. A huge chasm 8,000 feet deep and filled with a stone-streaked glacier divides us from the three Torres. They are three miles away, but seem as if I could hold them in my hands. Beyond the Torre massif lies the ice cap. The ice cap runs north and south to the limit of my vision, and whole unknown mountain ranges rise within it. Just beside us is the row of steep vertical cracks that furrow the North Face of Aguja Poincenot. East, the pyramid shadow of Fitzroy stretches for miles across light green and brown hills. The scene is impossibly enormous. I've got one foot in the next world.

I stand ramrod straight with my boot heels held together, spread my arms wide, and squeeze out a smile for the camera. I'm happy to be here, sure, but my overriding emotion is surprise. I am shocked. A faint, damp breeze tickles my nostrils and disturbs the loose straps that hang from my backpack. The breeze draws attention to the smudge of dirty gray, just visible, far away to the west between the sun and the ice cap. I don't need a weatherman to tell me that that smudge is the leading edge of a new storm.

Motohiko, the Japanese soloist, climbs up to join us on Fitzroy's summit. He's the first person ever to climb the Franco-Argentine Route without a partner. I'm in awe of the man's courage and I feel as surprised as he looks. Moto faces the plummeting sun and holds his good-luck headband up between his two upraised hands. One Slovenian, one Japanese, and one American on the summit of Fitzroy—an unlikely combination. The day is almost over and the other parties must be settling in to bivy, probably in spots where they can't see that smudge of cloud out west.

This one taste of Patagonia won't be nearly enough to last a lifetime. I take a long look at Cerro Torre. There, I tell myself, right there, that is my next mountain.

We take all night to get down from the top of Fitzroy. We rappel past the bergschrund and reach the glacier just as gray light oozes into the blackness, showing a layer of dark cloud that roars in from the west and buries the summits. Below the east side of La Brecha we're in a lee and out of the wind. More light filters into the world and we can see currents seethe and roil within the clouds as they storm off toward the rising sun. Moto collapses in the snow, too exhausted to take another step, and says he will wait for the next party down. Boris and I leave him there and set off down the glacier toward Paso Superior. Far off to the east the sun steps up to the horizon. Red and orange light beams shoot between the earth and storm and set our world on fire. Orange fire twists and writhes on the underside of storm. The bottom halves of the peaks around us burn yellow-red. Even the glacier tints pumpkin orange. The black figure of Boris stumbling through the snow in front of me looks like the figure of a pilgrim in hell. Neither of us has slept in four of the last six nights, and the whole scene has the hard edge of a hallucination.

•

A few days later an old Argentine couple gave me a lift out of Chaltén in their VW van. I bumped along on a bench seat in the back with my feet propped on my pack. I was clean, freshly showered, and relaxed as I stared out the window at the steppes and wind. Then with a *whooosh* and a *thump, thump, thump,* a tire went flat. I got out into the wind and broke my personal promise never to fix another VW. I jacked up the van and changed the flat. Behind, miles away, were the Andes. I could see Fitzroy, the sun low in the sky and the mountain's face dark and shadowed. Tall and slender Cerro Torre stood left of Fitzroy. I bent and stood and watched the mountains as I cleaned the grease from my hands with dirt and a tuft of brown grass. The far mountain rampart of Patagonia showed no detail, just the black outline of that other world. I had been there and back, another personal promise kept.

An hour later the fan belt broke and I had to fix that too.

That night in the town of El Calafate I met a woman carrying a plastic bag full of little *calafate* berries, for which the town is named. I peered into the bag. Legend has it that anyone who eats *calafate* berries in Patagonia is certain to return. I ate a handful.

Muchas gracias." I reach across the bench seat, shake hands, climb down from the cab, hoist my backpack out of the bed, and give the pickup's tailgate a slap. "*Suerte*," the old Chilean gaucho, his face as battered as his pickup, yells through the cab's back window. *Luck.* The dilapidated Ford bounces away south. I stand, buffeted by the wind, and watch him go. This is sheep country, and the bleak landscape resonates with a chord of buried memory. The land of my mother's family sheep farm in the foothills of the Welsh border felt alike in spirit, if not in fact.

The plume of dust torn away from the pickup's wheels by the fearsome west wind shimmers yellow in the low sunlight of the austral afternoon. My pack sits in the middle of the intersection. Strands of barbed wire flank all four unsurfaced roads. North and east, low hills roll away. South, far ahead of the truck bouncing into the distance, a snow-capped mountain range props up the sky. West, where I came from, the land slopes down to the shore and the road runs alongside the

tortured waters of Bahía Inútil (Useless Bay). Surges of wind charge
across the grasses and scrub brush of Tierra del Fuego.

Down all four roads is desolation. I'm trying to get to Ushuaia, the
southernmost city in the Argentine half of Tierra del Fuego, and it's
painfully obvious that no more vehicles are going to pass this day. Since
the Punta Arenas–to–Porvenir ferry doesn't run tomorrow, there isn't
likely to be any traffic then either. Thirty miles east is the Argentine
frontier, but at least the wind is at my back and it's not raining. I shoulder my pack and begin to walk.

My boots swallow the miles; my shadow lengthens. Endless
steppes surround me, the gentle hills like swells in a frozen sea. I follow the barbed wire east. Ahead, a dozen guanacos—the largest members of the llama family, resembling humpless camels—leap the fence,
cross the road, leap again, and disappear among the folds of earth to
the north. A gray owl perched on a fence post opposite fixes me with
black eyes. Enormous hares dash across the road, startled. The occasional fox darts among the tall grasses. The wind is strong, and constant. It's unspeakably lonely.

The sun sits on the horizon behind as I top a small crest. Before
me, nestled against a rise from the base of a shallow valley, are two
buildings. One is a fancy mansion; the other looks to be a bunkhouse.
Behind the latter a solitary figure chops wood. I close the distance on
an overgrown track from the road. The man stops, watches, and then
plants the head of his axe into a stump and comes toward me. The wind
isn't so bad in this dale. We shake hands. I ask for water.

The young man can scarce keep the wonder from his face as he
walks me to the bunkhouse. "Alfredo," he says in Spanish, "my name is
Alfredo." He can't yet be out of his teens, but he appears hardened in
his worn denim clothes. Alfredo dips my bottle into a bucket of water
and asks if I have a place to spend the night. To my negative reply he
says, "Then stay here, there is much space." I nod. "Put your things in

that room." By the time I return, Alfredo has dashed to the yard for an armload of split wood. He looks relieved when he returns—I didn't disappear.

Alfredo prepares mutton stew and spouts forth a steady stream of heavily accented Spanish. I have difficulty following and can only fish out the basic facts. He is from the island of Chiloé, off the Chilean coast far to the north. He is eighteen and very happy to have this work. As the new man he must keep the *estancia*'s buildings while the older men tend the herds; maybe next year he can work with them. The *estancia* has few cattle, but many, many sheep. He has never met the *estancia*'s owners. He loves racing horses. Alfredo hasn't spoken to another soul in a fortnight.

In gathering gloom we tear apart the hot mutton and homemade bread—by far the best meal cooked by a teenager I've ever had. After dinner we take warm milk to an orphaned calf. The calf nurses through a rubber nipple attached to a two-liter plastic bottle. When she's done, Alfredo starts a generator. Inside, he rams a straightened coat hanger into the antenna slot of a radio so old that it could have broadcast news of the Normandy invasion. Alfredo looks up to see if I approve, and we listen to melancholy tangos beamed from Argentina.

Out comes a bottle of fiery pisco, the Patagonian hard liquor of choice, and the conversation rages into the night. Alfredo talks about the horse he's going to buy with his season's wages. He treats me with great respect, almost deference, surprised at my questions. The amount of money I make per hour as a construction hand astounds him. Alfredo's eyes and manner betray his certainty in the enormous gulf of wealth, culture, and class that divides our lives.

In the morning, we rise with the sun and Alfredo cooks pancakes. I thank him profusely and heft my load, fueled for the journey. We shake hands and I descend the bunkhouse stairs and walk the track back to the road, where I stop and wave. Alfredo stands on the porch and raises his hand in turn. Across those two hundred yards I realize that the distance between his life and mine isn't enormous at all. One side of my family hails from the English countryside; only a generation separates me from life on a Shropshire sheep farm. And shepherds have no need of mountains.

B ACK IN BOULDER AFTER THAT FIRST TASTE OF Patagonian adventure I was faced with the final evaporation of the money I had saved as an Army officer. That magic hour on the summit of Fitzroy had fixed my next mountain goal— Cerro Torre—firmly in my mind, but expeditions far from home are time-consuming and expensive, and any alpinist who dreams of the world's great mountains needs money, a lot of money. It took a horrendous year of construction work to earn my return to Patagonia.

I first fell into residential construction working for a friend of a friend named Jules. I rented a slice of floor in a tiny house and fought for space with two huge, half-wild dogs. Since the only way to make good money earning wage is to stockpile hours, I supplemented the construction job with a gig on a snow-removal crew. I rejoiced when snowstorms buried Boulder. I would sortie at midnight into the falling snow with a snow blower, a shovel, and a thermos of black coffee, primed to throw snow for the rest of the night, for which I was paid cash under the table. Hell, so came the money from

Jules's barely afloat construction operation, but the money from Jules didn't come nearly as quick. Fast and furious snowstorms that struck with the sunset produced the best work binges. I would put in a full eight hours on one of Jules's remodeling jobs, then eat dinner at Taco Bell and sleep for three or four hours. At midnight I'd be at the snow-removal equipment shed ready for more labor. We'd have the necessary walkways, driveways, and steps cleared by eight or nine in the morning and I could go straight back to work pounding nails for Jules. I landed weekend jobs when the Boulder Rock Club needed an ice-climbing guide. I worked my ass off, and when my motivation flagged I dangled the Patagonian Andes in front of my mind's eye like a big, fat plum. Every dollar I salted away marked another small step toward Patagonia.

All was going according to plan when an intrusive and expensive girlfriend cost me the floor space, bled my modest stack of Cerro Torre savings dry, and racked up a big credit-card debt. I landed in the spare room of a North Boulder trailer park and fought myself free only after protracted emotional trench warfare. When that Verdun finally exhausted itself I was further from Cerro Torre than I had ever been. Then Jules's construction business collapsed. Two weeks of my wages went unpaid, and a month's worth of snowstorms never veered south of Canada. But amid the turmoil, when I didn't work, I climbed: Colorado ice and, on warm days, local rock. A pal and I pulled a winter ascent of the Longs Peak Diamond, a steep, bitter wall that rises to 14,000 feet in Rocky Mountain National Park, and he landed me a job with a heavy construction company out of Denver building a sewer lift station for the city of Loveland, Colorado. A sewer lift station—a device whose purpose is every bit as horrible as its name suggests—includes such aptly named components as a "sewage storage vault" and an "emergency overflow vault." One of the few blessings in my life at the time was that the job was new construction and not a retrofit. But the hours promised to be long, and in the absence of inclement weather each work week would stretch out into overtime, and time and a half is a hand's Holy Grail.

To build the lift station we had to sink the storage vault (a thirty-foot-tall, fourteen-foot-diameter concrete cylinder) into the ground, set the overflow vault (a concrete blockhouse the size of a single-car garage) underground beside it, install powerful pumps, and plumb the two vaults together, then link the whole setup to the existing sewer mains. We did a survey and then two front-end loaders scooped dirt into dump trucks and dug out a fifty-foot-square, sixteen-foot-deep, swimming-pool-like hole. A few feet down the loaders broke into the water table and we had to run heavy pneumatic mine pumps to stop the hole from turning into a Flanders quagmire. With the swimming pool dug we still had to sink a shaft another sixteen feet down in order to make a big enough hole to bury the full thirty-foot height of the main sewage storage vault. We struggled for two days to form and cement the outside of a six-foot-high, sixteen-foot-diameter doughnut of steel liner plate into level alignment in a shallow hole scraped into the bottom of the swimming pool. When the concrete set and fixed the metal ring in place, a backhoe crept down a dirt ramp into the bottom of the swimming pool and set to work from a perch at the rim of the steel cylinder. Liner plate stops a shaft from caving in on itself, and we had to bolt successive rings of plate to the bottom of the steel doughnut as the backhoe dug out the hole.

From its perch the backhoe sunk the cylinder deeper and deeper into the crumbly dirt, shale, and clay below Loveland. Ten feet down (and twenty-six feet below lawn level) the backhoe's scoop could make no further digging progress. The backhoe's bucket could still lift dirt out of the hole from that depth, but it couldn't dig. A six-foot-deep, sixteen-foot-diameter cylinder of dirt remained to be dug out of the bottom of the hole. It was up to three of us hands, armed with shovels and airspades, to finish the job. An airspade is a pneumatic tool similar to a jackhammer, except that an airspade is light enough to manipulate in directions other than straight down, maneuvers that can't possibly be made with a jackhammer. But like a jackhammer, an airspade is very, very loud, and combined with the racket of the pumps the noise was thunderous.

An M8 pneumatic mine pump is a red-orange contraption about the size of a lawn mower, although much lighter, and it makes a god-awful mechanical clank and whoosh as it labors. The pump labored and three of us, wearing hip waders, wet work clothes, and leather gloves, slaved away in the bottom of that pit—thumping out wet dirt and clay with the airspades and shoveling it into the backhoe bucket. High-pressure air hoses snaked around behind us and rose up and out into the circle of sky at the top of the hole. The noise inside that metal-lined cylinder was like the screaming of the damned. It jarred my bones. I wore earplugs under earphones, but the power, the raw energy of the sound that pounded back and forth in that metal-lined hole made my teeth ache and my eyes hurt.

A perverse pride permeates a good construction crew, pride that pushes you to be the one working the hardest, doing the nastiest job, getting the most done, being the dirtiest. Even the engineers and the supers aren't immune, and our two were regularly at the bottom of that pit, fighting to take their turn on the airspades.

For fifty hours that week I thrashed around in dirt and water at the bottom of the hole, wrestling with a bucking airspade, shoveling heavy dirt, or hoisting and bolting new rounds of liner plate into place. We dug the hole down to thirty-two feet, wet, beyond deaf, with aching backs and swollen hands. Saturday finally came, a beautiful Colorado winter Saturday, and almost warm sunshine beamed down through the pine needles onto the rocks of Flagstaff Mountain above Boulder— perfect conditions for a rock-climbing workout. I laced up my rock shoes in a patch of sunshine below my favorite traverse, stepped up to the stone, and discovered my hands were useless. They hurt too much to close over the biggest "jug" holds. My hands refused to climb. The wage was good, but it wasn't *that* good, and if I couldn't climb there was no point to the work. Working heavy construction was strictly climbing support. I desperately wanted to get back to Patagonia, and I needed money to do it, but I couldn't give up climbing in the meantime. Besides, if I didn't climb, I would be physically unfit for the action when I finally did get to Patagonia. I gave notice Monday morning.

I worked my remaining two weeks, and the work didn't get much easier. By the end of the second Friday, we were ready to hook the system up to the city's sewer mains and test it, but that was my last day, and I had no need to see our lift station work.

Monday I began a new job with a start-up company down in Colorado Springs, but the saga of the sewer lift station didn't end. Monday night my answering machine had a message from one of the other hands, roundly cussing me for a lucky bastard. I got out just in time. In a moment of operator negligence the trenching machine, a device like a massive chain saw that hacks a swath in the earth, went astray and busted a live sewer main. Vile sewage flooded the 200-foot-long ditch between our new construction and the sewer main. The crew had to pull on the hip waders one last time and wade around in the raw stuff while they stopped the break, cleaned the grotesque mess, assembled the last of the new pipeline, and made a clean hookup to Loveland's sewers.

I suffered much blue-collar humiliation for Cerro Torre, but at least I avoided trial by cesspool. My mountain dream was in such tight focus that I probably would have waded through shit to get there. Only with the dream in such sharp focus could I manage the details of my ten-dollar-a-day existence. I lived in a spare room in a trailer park. In Boulder I was a regular at the Gondolier's once-a-week three-dollar all-you-can-eat pasta feed and at the Dark Horse's beer-and-hamburger-for-less-than-five-bucks night. I connected the days between with frequent feeds at Taco Bell. I never went to the movies. If I drank, I drank strong drinks at the cheapest bars. I dutch-dated with a girlfriend as tightfisted as me, and I climbed with old, ratty gear.

•

My new job was the brainchild of Phil Krichilsky, one of my best West Point friends and an old climbing partner. Phil's not a natural climber—he struggles for every inch—but he's a natural business-man. Phil mustered out of the Army from Colorado Springs deter-mined to build a successful business. He had no money saved and no line of credit to tap, but Phil had a plan, albeit a very strange one.

There is a whole industry that builds, installs, and services the massive indoor play structures that you see in fast-food restaurants. Kids love exploring the plastic tubes and jumping around in the net-enclosed pits filled with hollow plastic balls. But with dozens of kids loose inside every day, sanitation often suffers, and cleaning the ball pits is a big, labor-intensive job.

Before he left the Army Phil had seen a system rigged to a ball pit that piqued his interest. A bull's-eye with a hole in the middle was bolted between two vertical supports. Kids spontaneously threw balls at the target. When they got a dead-center hit the balls went through the target and into a machine designed to wash and return the balls to the pit. The device was jammed 99 percent of the time, but Phil appreciated the beauty of the idea, despite the poor execution. By throwing balls into the target the kids—clients of the restaurants—

were actually doing work. The kids were cleaning the balls. Phil located the guy who had built the ball washer, and they went into business together. Phil was soon running the show. The whole operation was done by the seat of Phil's pants, but it was seat of the pants *done well*. Phil enlisted the help of Franklin J. Macon, a seventy-five-year-old Tuskegee airman, and a man who can turn sows' ears into silk purses if he has the right set of tools.

Frank, Phil, and I tinkered around with the machine as we tried to design, build, and market a functional ball washer. The final device, christened "the FunWash," was a zany work of art. Its plastic case was about the size of two washing machines, and Frank rigged a series of Granger catalog parts inside the box to stir, wash, and move balls. A squirrel-cage fan at the end of the wash rack shot the cleaned balls fifteen feet up a tube of PVC pipe and the balls emerged onto an aerial train track. Gravity rolled the balls down the track until they dropped through the roof of the ball pit.

There was a measure of respect to be earned as a heavy construction hand. None could be gleaned from work as a ball washer, and my tough-guy climber buddies handed me unmerciful abuse over the new job. But the pay was better, the work wasn't as crucifying, and none of the humor of the endeavor was lost on Phil, Frank, and me, which was crucial, because every aspect of the FunWash business was a headache. Phil worked himself to the bone. His wife, Mary Beth, was pregnant, and his family's survival depended on the success of the enterprise. Phil ran the operation while Frank built each machine, and I installed them. Each install was a custom fiddlefest of tweak and re-tweak that only I seemed to have the patience to endure.

Summer came and went. The low points were a series of jobs in sweltering Orlando, the flattest place on earth. On into the autumn I drove to jobs in Colorado, Nebraska, Texas, Utah, Nevada, Missouri, and Illinois. I flew to jobs in New York, California, and Venezuela. November came and I sortied to a trio of jobs in Moorehead, Minnesota; Milwaukee, Wisconsin; and some little town in southern Ohio. I tightened the last bolt in Ohio, showed the locals how to clean and use the FunWash, and pushed west on I-70 through wind and snow to Colorado. I loaded my duffels, moved out of the trailer, strip-mined my savings account, and flew to South America, my dream dragged out from under the shit pile of that life. I went back to Patagonia and I climbed Cerro Torre.

•

I was in South America for nearly five months: the first three in Patagonia, a month spent climbing rock in Bariloche, and the last weeks spent visiting friends and touring in northeastern Argentina and in Uruguay. My sixty-eight-day campaign to climb the Compressor Route was the best time of my life so far. The pain was real, and extreme, and months would pass before I could again handle serious suffering, but I had lived ten weeks without compromise. I had lived in absolute concert with my desires. Reality had exceeded the dream.

By the time I got back to Colorado I was flat-assed broke, and I went straight back to work for Phil. Phil had diversified while I was away to include cleaning and maintaining entire playgrounds. Business was booming, and I had to learn the new job. It took about an hour.

For the next six months I cleaned indoor playgrounds and installed ball washers all over the country. I hated the "tune-ups," as we called the cleanings, and every morning the jobs got harder and harder to stomach.

Meltdown came one morning in suburban Denver. At six A.M., I met the assistant manager. She couldn't understand why I was there that day. Her minimum-wage teenagers had cleaned the playground yesterday and it didn't need another cleaning. She had personally inspected it. She didn't even offer me a cup of coffee. I bought one (the last dollar I have spent in that fast-food chain). I took one look at the stretched seams of her polyester uniform and knew for a God-given fact that that assistant manager had not crawled around inside the play structure because she could never fit down the plastic tubes. I convinced her that her owner did, in fact, want us to "tune up" the playland. She insisted that I get done before the lunch rush. That big plastic baby-sitter was way too good for business to have it closed through lunch.

I crawled in with my tools and cleaning supplies. Crushed french fries caulked plastic seams. Half hamburgers lived underneath some of the knee pads. Ketchup finger paintings decorated the interior walls. I'd be lucky if I could clean this disaster before midnight.

By nine-thirty, I was covered with such filth that I had the taste of stale fast food on my teeth, and I told the assistant manager that I'd have to keep the playland closed all day. I got out for a refill of coffee and a perusal of the sports page to lower my blood pressure. "It's just a job," I told myself as I tried to summon the bile for another foray into playland. Suddenly the fat assistant manager appeared and berated me for not working and told me to get out of her restaurant. I was speechless, agog, and writhing with humiliation.

I found my voice: "Lady, this play structure is a health hazard, but since you don't care, I don't either. I'll be out of here in a second."

I called Phil from the parking lot pay phone. He had just gotten an earful of the same abuse from the same assistant manager.

"Phil, you do know why she threw me out, right?"

"Other than the fact that you're a pain in the ass?"

"Because she didn't want to cut into the lunchtime sales on her shift, and they'd have gotten battered with the playland closed. No amount of money is worth this shit. Don't sign me up for any more of these jobs."

Phil had the good sense not to argue.

That day was the nadir of the long descent that swept me down from the summit of Cerro Torre. I handed the toolbox back to Phil and embraced my oldest dream, a dream I had held since I first learned to read. I had decided to write for a living. With that stunt I kicked the last vestige of certainty out of my life. I hoped I'd find something to say. Soon, I was in Patagonia again.

LA TIERRA DESCONOCIDA:

THE UNKNOWN COUNTRY

CHANGE IS A FACT OF OUR WORLD LIKE THE sunrise, and the cosmologists tell us even that won't happen forever. In the mountains, the wide rivers of ice, so seemingly motionless, move, full of turbulence and eddies and rapids and runs. Man seldom sees the glaciers move, but to the great granite obelisks the torrents of ice must pass in a wild frozen blur. Even the mountains themselves change, albeit at the pace of continental drift, shedding a layer of skin here, the blemish of a few boulders there, not appreciably smaller, but never quite the same. In our constant struggle to create security in a chaotic universe, most humans take root, set their feet in stone, and fight change. But change is a most implacable foe, one certain to sweep even his most conservative opponent into unknown seas. I embraced another big change nine months after Cerro Torre and right before I returned to Patagonia—I got married. Three Patagonian expeditions had taught me the value of opportunity, and DeAnne was my golden one. With her I share the ultimate base camp.

•

In mid-November, Jim Donini and I came to Patagonia intent on bagging a new route, fixed on climbing a mountain feature that had never been ascended before. Jim had made stacks of alpine first ascents; I'd made only one, which Jim and I scored together in the Alaska Range, a wild ride up the South Face of Mt. Bradley in the Ruth Gorge near Mt. McKinley. Except possibly in the case of an established route that has acquired a reputation as a terrifying and dangerous horror show, first ascents are more complicated and intimidating than repeats. Every detail of a first ascent is harder. Fear of the unknown bears down on the minds of first ascensionists. They have no topo—the detailed sketch that maps an established climb—which makes accurate planning difficult. An inadequate supply of hardware can halt an ascent, and not knowing what obstacles lie ahead tends to make climbers take more hardware for a wider variety of crack sizes. More equipment means more weight, which means climbing slower, which in itself requires a larger supply of equipment (food, clothing, stoves, fuel, perhaps bivy gear). And as alpinists try to ferret out a viable line of ascent up unknown terrain it is easy to choose the wrong way and climb into a vertical cul-de-sac with no way to continue above. In my last two southern seasons I'd got myself out from under the spell of the two greatest Patagonian summits, so this year I was free to blaze my own trail, and I screwed up my courage enough to try.

Storms raged for seventeen days after we arrived. Torrents of rain fell on base camp and nobody went climbing. Standard operating procedure in Patagonia. Finally, there was a half-day lull. Jim and I humped ropes, hardware, a tent, and two weeks of supplies up to a camp high in the cirque across from Cerro Torre and directly below Torre Innominata, determined to get some good weather.

Approaching the Compressor Route, which generally follows the left skyline, then blasts up the middle of the final headwall. © THOMAS ULRICH

Crouch rejected by a storm from the Compressor Route.

© ALEX HALL

Jim Donini, Stefan Hiermaier, and Greg Crouch in base camp.

© CHARLIE FOWLER

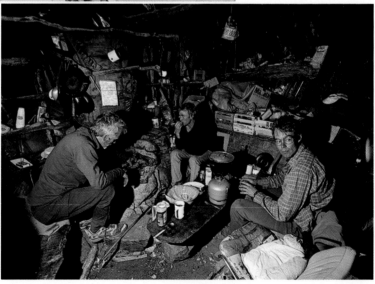

Charlie Fowler on the Compressor Route. © GREGORY CROUCH

Charlie Fowler climbing through the ice tower on the Compressor Route.

© GREGORY CROUCH

Charlie Fowler's feet on Maestri's compressor, Crouch in the mists below.

© CHARLIE FOWLER

The shadows of the Torres on the ice cap from the summit of Cerro Torre.

© GREGORY CROUCH

Crouch under the Torre's summit mushroom at sunrise. The crevasse where he and Fowler bivouacked is right behind his heels.

© CHARLIE FOWLER

Jim Donini climbing on the North Face of Aguja Poincenot. © GREGORY CROUCH

Donini's battered hands after climbing Poincenot.
© GREGORY CROUCH

The North Face of Aguja Poincenot.
© CHARLIE FOWLER

Crouch climbs a quarter of the way up Poincenot's North Face. © JIM DONINI

An estancia in winter.

© GREGORY CROUCH

Carrying loads through a storm. © THOMAS ULRICH

Climbing at sunset low on the West Face during the unsuccessful attempt. © THOMAS ULRICH

Gobsmacked while dragging the sleds
into the Cirque of the Altars.

© THOMAS ULRICH

Stefan Siegrist leads above the
Col of Hope. © THOMAS ULRICH

Stefan Siegrist, David Fasel, and Greg Crouch playing cards in the tent
during a storm day. © THOMAS ULRICH

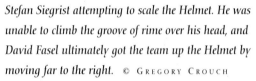

Stefan Siegrist attempting to scale the Helmet. He was unable to climb the groove of rime over his head, and David Fasel ultimately got the team up the Helmet by moving far to the right. © GREGORY CROUCH

Thomi Ulrich climbs a hard rock and ice in the upper dihedral of the West Face. © GREGORY CROUCH

Bivouac
The Headwall
The Helmet
Bivouac
Col of Conquest
The Col of Hope

Dotted line represents portion of route located behind the ridge shown here.

The West Faces of the Torres in winter. © GREGORY CROUCH

Stefan Siegrist leads up to the base of the Torre's summit mushrooms.

© THOMAS ULRICH

Stefan Siegrist leads a rime groove 200 feet below the top of Cerro Torre with Fitzroy beyond.
© THOMAS ULRICH

The Boys on Top: Thomas Ulrich, David Fasel (holding the ice ax), Stefan Siegrist,
Greg Crouch. © THOMAS ULRICH

David Fasel retreats with wind scouring the snow ridges in the background. © THOMAS ULRICH
Inset: *David Fasel at night during the stormy retreat.* © THOMAS ULRICH

Jim Donini on top of the West Pillar of Cerro Pollone, Cerro Torre under his right hand, the West Face of Piergiorgio behind his left knee, and the ice cap beyond. © GREGORY CROUCH

Greg Crouch a few hundred feet below the summit of the West Pillar of Cerro Pollone with Cerro Torre in the distance (the Compressor Route is the left profile of the Torre). © GREGORY CROUCH

J. Jay Brooks retreats from the West Face of Aguja Saint-Exupéry through a swirl of blowing snow. © GREGORY CROUCH

That evening, renewed wind, rain, and snow pelted our tent, and the dull, bass roar of the gale poured through the cols thousands of feet above us. Jim and I read, ate, slept, and told stories for the next four days. The view of towering granite spires through the tent flap ought to have been one of the best in the world, but through driving sheets of rain and snow I couldn't see 100 feet.

.

On our fourth afternoon at high camp, there looks to be hope for improving weather, and Doug Byerly and Rolando Garibotti appear at our tent flap. Like us, they're poised for an alpine binge on the Fitzroy massif. Jim and I usually roll our eyes at superambitious Patagonian aspirants, but Byerly tells us he once waited an entire month in Alaska's Kichatna Spires without a single climbing day, so it's obvious this first-timer has the right stuff. Rolo has been climbing in Patagonia for more than a decade. Both are proven climbers of astonishing ability. Rolo is simply the best of those of us obsessed with Patagonian alpinism.

An Argentine who grew up in Bariloche but carries an Italian passport and is married to an American, Rolo is *the man* here in Patagonia. Rolo's mail may be delivered in Boulder, Colorado, but he's seldom there to get it as he travels in long orbits between Europe, Colorado, Yosemite, Wyoming, and Argentina. He has the good characteristics of the Latin stereotype on abundant display. Rolo is warm, friendly and open, tall, dark, handsome, and hard-core, but utterly without a macho peacock's attitude. He's quietly competent and tough, or perhaps he's just so goddamned good that he has no need to display it. Rolo praises the people he admires, gets psyched for the accomplishments of his friends, and doesn't seem to have an envious bone in his six-feet-one-inch frame. I believe Rolo is megacompetitive—nobody that good isn't—but his competitiveness isn't rooted in a desire to see other people fail. Rolo uses his competitive fire to put the whip to himself, probably too much, but I think he has that fire so well internalized that the rest of the world only infrequently glimpses the white-hot blaze. Of all the climbers (even people) that I know, I don't think I admire anyone more than Rolando Garibotti as he quietly does his own thing and strives to make himself better, and the alpine compliment I covet most in the world is Rolo's terse "Good effort." It's not lightly given.

All night I am conscious of the absence of wind. A weak part of me—and not a small part—craves its return. I feel a flush of hope with every tiny breeze that ruffles the tent fabric. What few dreams I have in my half sleep flood me with fear, and the night passes dreadfully slow.

Beep, beep, beep . . .

And I wish it would go on forever as the alarm sounds.

I let my wristwatch alarm beep out all thirty pulses as Jim continues to snore. I feel like someone drove a stake through my heart and set my legs in concrete. Cold air filters through the tightly drawn top of my sleeping bag. Above us in the darkness stands the mountain we plan to climb. It's the shortest approach in the range from this camp to its base, but it's still a substantial uphill trudge over talus and snow. Jim will be none the wiser if I go back to sleep and claim that I didn't hear the alarm. If I do that, we'll wake with the sun and have to put off our project for another day. Sleep, delicious sleep; it's the only luxury in the world for me right now. Seductive sleep pulls at my mind, but then my one fear larger than my fear of the mountain nauseates me—my fear of being a coward—and that fear gets me to fumble with the mummy cord of my sleeping bag. I fight my head out into the cold, dark night and grab around for my headlamp.

"Get up."

"Ugh . . . coffee."

Lured by two beautiful parallel cracks clearly visible through our tent door, we are drawn to attempt the unclimbed West Ridge of Torre Innominata as a warm-up climb. It's an obvious route, but like so much here in Patagonia, it has never been climbed before. Donini and I undertake the climb with two and a half liters of water, four Snickers bars apiece, and no bivy gear. We think that the West Ridge of Innominata, which looks tiny wedged between the giants of Poincenot and Saint-Exupéry, will climb easily, and in a day.

Difficult mixed climbing and awkward horizontal route finding don't go easily, or in a day, and thirty-six hours and one bitterly cold open bivy later we do a short rappel from the end of our twenty-fourth pitch to the notch where the 1974 British Route joins the West Ridge. The long, wet storm that kept us tentbound had packed most of Innominata's cracks with ice, and we climbed at a glacial pace. Six pitches remain to the summit and success. Donini takes himself off rappel, doubles over, and dry heaves. His dehydration and exhaustion have worsened through the day, and he convulses after every exertion. I have a blinding headache. We debate whether to continue. Neither of us has the stomach for another bivy away from sleeping bags or to descend through darkness over unknown terrain, yet my first Patagonian "first" lies six pitches out of my grasp. Reluctantly, we retreat to camp with the remaining daylight.

Innominata, whose name means "without name" in Spanish, had served up a route the size of Yosemite's El Capitan. We had grossly underestimated its wallop, dwarfed as it is by the spires to either side. Innominata has another name on official documents, Aguja Rafael or something, but I've never heard a climber call it anything besides Innominata, and so unnamed it shall remain.

Most every committed climber fails in Patagonia because of bad weather, but we failed on Innominata under a deep blue and windless sky. If we'd brought sleeping bags, or a stove, we would have bagged a Patagonian first ascent, a dream I've held for years. The fiasco crushes me. We journeyed all this way to the southern tip of South America, spent three thousand dollars apiece on travel and equipment, and, amid perfect weather, stomped ourselves with stupidity. We don't deserve a second chance.

•

Jim and I are awake and brewing coffee the next morning when Doug and Rolo stumble back into camp. While we were up there getting schooled, they peeled off two summits. The British Route on Innominata the first day of the good spell, and then late yesterday morning, as we were struggling sideways like ungainly crabs on icy and awkward horizontal terrain, we saw them down at the base of Saint-Exupéry. I figured Doug and Rolo were either fixing the bottom few hard mixed pitches on Chiaro di Luna (a route on Saint-Exu's West Face) or were planning to spend the night on the climb. A "crack of noon" start is hardly standard alpine practice.

In the late evening, as Jim and I passed the base of Innominata on our way down, we saw Doug and Rolo again, two small dots way up near the top of Saint-Exupéry. Enough light remained for them to make the summit before dark. They cracked off the second ascent of a 3,000-foot alpine wall, and they completed the twenty-eight pitches after starting at eleven A.M. I'm impressed!

The weather holds. Fed and rehydrated, Jim and I feel okay. We need a new project. We want a face this time—a route with a plumb vertical line. We don't want to grapple with more of the horizontal climbing that plagued us on Innominata. Rolo thinks we should try some cracks on Aguja Poincenot's North Face that he saw a few years ago. The remote North Face of Aguja Poincenot, the sexy stone needle that stands next to Fitzroy, is visible from no civilized place, not from any base camp or our high camp. Few people have ever seen it; no one has ever attempted to climb it. I enthusiastically recall my view of the face from the summit of Fitzroy. Rolo's right, I think, that's prime terrain! Jim and I give each other the eye, nod, and begin loading gear.

The sleeping bags and the stove go into our packs this time.

Due to the accident of mountain architecture that makes it impossible to get a decent view of the North Face of Poincenot from anywhere on the valley floor, we won't be able to scope a specific route until we're up into a little pocket ice-field amphitheater that hangs at the base of the North Face between Poincenot itself, the obscure spire of Aguja Desmochada, and the southern flank of Fitzroy. It'll cost us more than 4,000 feet of elevation gain and much traversing to unravel the arduous, technical, and in some places objectively dangerous approach to that little amphitheater. Just going up there is a big leap of faith—in ourselves, in the climbability of an unknown Patagonian mountain wall, and in Rolo's advice, but in the last two cases, I'm sure our faith is well placed.

Early the next morning Jim and I stand to the side of the pocket ice field in a spot we figure isn't too badly threatened by the seracs poised to pitch over a cliff band at the upper end of our amphitheater and annihilate anything in the middle of the ice field. We have to cross directly underneath that serac band to reach the base of Poincenot, but the slope is easy and we should get across quickly. We stand and examine the face—more than 2,000 feet of brown, gray, and yellow granite split by many vertical crack systems. Rolo was right: This face looks fabulous, and steep, and pretty hard. Both Jim and I are serious granite aficionados, and we plainly see a gold mine of unclimbed granite rising in front of us. We examine and discuss the various crack systems, a visual reconnaissance aimed at increasing our store of foreknowledge before we commit to ascent. We scrutinize potential lines of ascent for connecting cracks, the weak lines of the mountain's defense. Some cracks look too wide. Others start well, but then die out in blank seas of vertical granite. A couple look pretty good, but there's no way to know exactly what the cracks up there are like. Preknowledge is never wholly accurate, and surprise lurks at every turn. Not knowing induces powerful fear, but this fear is a rare and precious spice, and I'm on the verge of a smile as we hash over the various merits of each possible line.

Our process of route selection is an effort to merge the dream of a potential route with the reality of our own capabilities. It's very easy to imagine bagging routes and summits in Patagonia while looking at drawings and photos of the range spread out on a table back home. Many people, well versed in tearing through the terrain of their home turf, arrive in Patagonia full of hugely ambitious dreams, most of them destined to remain fantasies. If Jim and I overestimate our abilities and underestimate Patagonia (as we just did on Innominata), we'll end up like the one member of a team who came south wildly spewing the motto of their first-ever trip to Patagonia to anyone who would listen: "Two men, three towers, one season." Harsh Patagonian reality reduced that motto to "Two men, one season, no towers." I really want to make sure that doesn't happen to me. But if we dwell too much on the realities of the situation, we won't have the guts to try. Having set out to do something that hasn't yet been done, we strive to strike the perfect balance between dream and reality and then to take a methodical approach to doing it.

We opt for what seems to be a continuous system of vertical cracks, corners, and chimneys just right of center. We plan to leave the ice field near the bottom right-hand side of the face and climb a huge, right-facing corner that goes up and leans left for a few hundred feet to arrive at the right edge of a broad ledge. From the ledge we'll blast up some thin cracks and corners that split the main part of the face and should take us to about half height. Above halfway we can't make out much detail, but there look to be possibilities, although we could well be wrong. Indeed, we have no certain knowledge that our crack system will prove climbable, but the only way to find out is to try, and we're game for that.

"The bottom looks good to me," says Jim, "and we should be able to figure something out above there that'll get us to the top."

"Yep, let's get after it."

A journey into the unknown may begin with such a single step, but popular wisdom has it wrong: the first steps aren't the most difficult ones. It's much harder to stay the course, and the most difficult steps are the ones that take you up and through the breach of commitment, that physical, mental, or emotional sticking point from which one cannot easily back away. On each separate climb I discover some point, some pitch, some section that ratchets me up to the sticking point and forces me through that breach. With those steps I leave the world behind and pin myself onto the leading edge of ascent. The summit isn't assured once I get through the breach, but success is, assuming everybody survives. Through the breach, my fear shifts from vague apprehensions and excuses that pull me down to the safe world below, into something almost rational, a fear that lives in the cold assessment of an evolving situation. The fear remains—I wouldn't climb without it—but the excuses have been trimmed like so much fat from a fresh, bloody carcass. The breach of full commitment is hard to find, it's different on every mountain, but once through the breach I'm abandoned to the full power of my desire. And breathing deep of that rarefied air beyond the breach is the place I want to be, even if in my cowardice I actively eschew such moments of total commitment.

·

I belay and follow Jim for the first three or four pitches to the big ledge. I look up the rope to Jim, and the huge wall towers over his head. Yellow granite rises into the sky and the vertical cracks seem to converge at the summit in the distance. The sun is still behind the summit, but half of a huge circular halo rings the top of the tower, the halo around the sun caused by light refracted through ice crystals in the upper atmosphere. Odds are those ice crystals are formed from moisture pushed out ahead of an onrushing storm.

Three or four hours later I've completed my block of leads, and we're another six or eight hundred feet up. The wind is blowing, a cloud cap has swallowed the summit of Fitzroy, the temperatures are plummeting, and it's hard to ignore the fact that a storm is coming on. The gut-grinding howl of the wind rises over the top of Fitzroy, but, oddly, the wind is out of the north. On the North Face of Poincenot we are in Fitzroy's wind shadow. Yet, with a storm on the march, we need a bivy, and fast.

I scramble up a pitch to the top of a sloping ledge and scope some bivy possibilities on a rock tower to the right. Jim climbs the rope with his ascenders, schlepping up the load, while I rappel and pendulum over on the slack of the fixed rope to check the sites. One is too small, but the other will do. We shuttle our gear over amid snow flurries and wild gusts. I prepare the site while Jim chops ice from a block perched beside us and hoards the shards in a stash behind a flake, where they'll serve as our water cache. We make a floor of sleeping pads, ropes, and backpacks and wedge into bivy sacks and sleeping bags. The ledge is one person wide, and only about a person and a half long, but it has good slope and tilts us back toward the solid rock instead of pitching us out into the void. It'll work if we put our heads at opposite ends and overlap our feet in the middle.

"Cup of potato flakes?" I ask, exhausted all of a sudden.

"Sounds great."

We sit in our bags, dangle our feet over the drop, and use the ends of our sleeping pads to make a shelter for the stove. While the water heats I do a quick inventory of our food.

"Hey, Jim, how dumb do you think we are?"

"Pretty dumb, why?"

"Because we're gonna run out of food again. These flakes for tonight, and then only some candy bars and another bag of potato flakes. We don't even have a teabag." I cuss us roundly for idiots.

Visibility comes and goes, clouds and snow flurries race through the cols between the peaks. The dull roar of the north wind still grinds over the top of Fitzroy. Local gusts crack loud and sharp as they attack our lonely ledge high on this wild Patagonian wall. When the local gusts abate, snowflakes pile up on our bivy sacks. Then resurgent gusts drive the flakes into the little breathing holes out of which Jim and I poke our noses. We howl and cheer at the strongest gusts.

"We're squarely in harm's way again," I say to Jim.

"This feels like a wanker storm, though. I've never seen a storm from the north before."

"Me neither, but if the wind swings around to the west we're gonna get smoked."

The gray slowly turns to black as night falls. I try to stay warm in my old, loftless sleeping bag wearing every stitch of clothing I have, including my storm gear and two hats. Gusts batter our aerie. I mentally rehearse the specifics of descent in case the storm goes ballistic and we can't ride it out. I know where and with what I'll build each anchor, and the rehearsal does much to assuage my fear. I'm confident that we can retreat from this ledge without a consequence more serious than discomfort, and neither of us cares too much about that. Inside my bivy sack in the dark I fight a constant war to keep my nose lined up with the two-inch airhole I keep in the zipper.

No stars are visible the few times I risk a glance outside the sack.

The night is jet-black. Only the periphery of my vision can discern the edges of the great peaks against the inky sky. I trace out the shapes in the dark, and the massive bulks of stone and ice seem to stand in the coal-black night like a vast heavenly tribunal, hunkered down against time and divided from me by an impenetrable void. We are here, proud and alone, but of all the tortures meted out to man, this is the hardest to bear: that the universe doesn't care. The universe is utterly unmoved by the human condition, and a god's wrath would be a much easier burden than the eternal indifference apparent in this black night.

At dawn it's still cold, gusty, cloudy, and definitely not a climbing day. There's nothing to do except wait. A stratum of soft medium gray laminates the sky, a cloud layer so monochromatic and of such uniform texture that in it I can discern no motion at all. At lower altitudes in the middle distance random chunks of darker gray run in from the ice cap and rove between the peaks of Domo Blanco, Piergiorgio, and Cerro Pollone. Occasional clouds whip around Poincenot and wrap us in a world of translucent gray, but the gray blur never quite eliminates the view to the vertiginous landscape beyond. Horizontal snow flurries streak through the hanging horseshoe valley between us, on Poincenot, and Desmochada, de la Silla, and Fitzroy. To the west, the low end of the horseshoe opens into the megavalley between the Torres and the Fitzroy massif, a drop so precipitous that we can't see much of the glacier in the valley floor.

We daydream and doze away the day, accompanied by the sound of the wind. Only occasional flurries of conversation break out, sparked by a comment like "There's a patch of blue behind Fitzroy." We're obsessed by the weather and note the most minute changes. I'd count this as a rest day if we had enough to eat, but all we have left are two candy bars apiece for today, and an energy bar each and a packet of instant mashed potatoes to share tomorrow morning. We'll either have to go up or fail again tomorrow. Jim's feet dig into my guts and ribs, and my feet dig into his. It's hardly comfortable, but it's not that bad, just another minor dose of alpine misery.

"This is bullshit," blurts Jim, perhaps touched by a little anemomania—wind madness. "This sport sucks. In my next life I'm playing baseball. Those sons-of-bitches get paid millions of dollars for playing a kid's game. I bet my ass every time I get on one of these granite tombstones and I don't get paid a goddamned dime. Fuck this."

I look at Donini's gaunt, gray-bewhiskered face tightly wrapped in a balaclava where it pokes out from his sleeping bag. I'm laughing, and I don't need a mirror to tell me that my appearance is just as dire. We're way off the leash, and Jim's only kidding to pass the time.

Thin clouds like skim milk whip through the high pass that separates Poincenot and Fitzroy. Our isolation boggles my mind. I finger my wedding ring, which I've got tied on a string around my neck, to remind myself that I've got a tie to the rest of the human race.

The second night is much, much colder. A sheen of ice forms inside my sleeping bag. I dream, awake and asleep, of being warm and comfortable back in Colorado with my wonderful bride. Fantasy and cold reality could hardly be more diametrically opposed. By dawn the wind isn't so bad, but our hands and feet would freeze if we tried rock climbing. We eat the last of our food and drink the tepid water left over from the potato flakes. After thirty-six hours without once losing contact with our sleeping pads we break the bivy and descend. We rig rappels for 1,000 feet to the base of the North Face and then down climb the convoluted 4,300-foot approach to high camp.

"We are going back to bag that route," Jim says as we near the tent. "That's the best alpine granite I've been on in thirty years."

I'm exhausted and all I want is a hot pot of tea and a letter from my wife.

By early afternoon when we get to our tent, the storm is breaking.

We'll be going up again tomorrow at first light if the weather trend continues. I feel like a yo-yo.

Jim and I eat and drink and prepare our next push. Six days of action have taken their toll on our supplies of hill food. Our gear is hammered. I chop up a nine-millimeter rope to make slings to replace our lightweight ones we left on Innominata and in the retreat from Poincenot. They're heavy and bulky, but they'll do. I'm sawing rope with a steak knife when Doug and Rolo tromp back into camp. Rolo has a letter from my wife that he picked up in Chaltén.

Doug and Rolo have been relaxing in base camp while Jim and I were up on the ledge, and their sights are set on Tehuelche, a forty-six-pitch route done on the North Face of Fitzroy by an Italian team a decade ago. It's one of the longest routes in Patagonia, and Rolo has dreamed of this route since he stole the original route topo from park headquarters when he was sixteen. The Italians fixed rope to within a few hundred feet of the summit in a siege campaign that lasted an entire season. The route has not had a second ascent, but Doug and Rolo plan to knock off Tehuelche in an overnighter.

I can't sleep and I listen to kernels of graupel snow beating against the tent. When I look out of the tent flap, clouds hang over Fitzroy, Poincenot, and Saint-Exupéry, and snow falls from them on our camp, but there are no clouds over the Torres on the western side of the valley, the side of the valley the weather usually bores in from. More weird weather; I've invested six months of my life and thirteen thousand dollars in this range and I still have no clue what the weather is going to do next. It snows most of the night, but the wind doesn't blow.

At four A.M. the strange clouds dissipate and I fire the stove to heat water. Jim groans. We're out of coffee. Once Jim gets going he's unstoppable, but it is essential to ply him with caffeine to fire his engines.

I find a few grit-covered tea bags in a corner of the tent. They'll have to do.

My body craves a rest day. We've been seriously pushing our envelope for seven days, but in Patagonia there is no tomorrow—it might rain and the wind might blow—and half measures don't ascend. We will push ahead until our bodies fail or a storm stops us.

We depart five minutes after Doug and Rolo begin their long approach to the North Face of Fitzroy. A massive snow gully; two steep steps of iced-up rock; a long, exposed snow traverse; another icy rock step; and a mad dash up and across that hanging defile threatened by seracs separates us from the base of Poincenot's North Face. It's yet another gut check for Jim and me, and I must concentrate to make every single step. Ambition is a harsh mistress, and I'm plumbing the bottom of my tank, but it's not Patagonia unless you hang on the cross for a while.

After several hours of slogging and scrambling we pause to drink warm tea and munch chocolate bars. Fortified, we crampon up the long, rising snow traverse. Jim is ahead of me, kicking steps through a crust of frozen snow under a heavy load. Jim is some kind of alpine Methuselah, much more interested in the climbing that he's going to do today and tomorrow than in the climbing he did yesterday. He's fifty-three years old and forging upward. I'm thirty and my thighs are burning.

We're not moving very fast, and it takes us until noon to reach the base of the climb. Snow and ice from last night's dump fill the cracks. The four rope lengths of Jim's lead are in a big, shady corner, and the sun's rays don't strike it, so the ice doesn't melt off. Jim hacks the cracks free of ice with his ice hammer and wedges his hands and feet into the cold fissures. Our progress is torturous and we reach a ledge atop the fourth pitch at six P.M., hours later than we had hoped.

Enough light remains to fix our ropes above the ledge. I lead the next section, just as on our first attempt. The sun has been on this stone, and it's mostly dry and free of ice. I'm in heaven as I romp up three pitches of continuous cracks that split the coarse yellow granite in front of me. These perfect, untouched cracks would hold their own in Yosemite, the international gold standard for granite crack climbs. The world is good; I am climbing inside my own dream, the only person in the history of the human race to touch this stone. A few final moves take me around a large square-cut roof to an anchor we left during our previous retreat. From there our two ropes should just stretch down to the broad ledge. I tie the ropes to the anchor and Jim and I rappel down to the ledge.

Back on the ledge we get through our standard dinner of noodles, butter, and tuna, and lay out our sleeping gear. I'm way too far gone to care what the food tastes like.

The sun is down by the time we finish dinner, and the long Patagonian summer evening stretches into night. The throaty rumble of a far-off avalanche echoes through the Andes. The Torres to the west are black silhouettes against a field of dark gray and purple-black in the giant horseshoe made by the black walls of Desmochada and Poincenot. Cocooned in his sleeping bag and bivy sack, Donini leans his back against a boulder and watches the light dim out of the sky. He props his insulated cup up in front of his chest, the cup full of his share of the starch and salt water left over from boiling our pasta. Jim holds the cup up in front of him with both hands, like an offering. The gray to the west could well prove ominous. The only starshine is in our half of the sky.

Seven consecutive days in the fray, twice thwarted, and with all my heart I want to see the summit of Aguja Poincenot. Hope is my rope, I love it and I hate it. And it changes nothing.

"Could go either way," I venture out into the gloom.

Jim's craggy features are hidden under his balaclava, and the dark wall of Poincenot soars above. He exudes Oriental calm. Jim takes a slow sip of his bilgewater and tosses the remains out onto the ledge.

"Fuck the weather, go to sleep."

And for the first time, I'm too exhausted for the torture of hope, fear, and desire. My demons rest, and I sleep well.

•

A thin, high layer of gray obscures the sky at dawn, but there's no wind.

"Good enough," says Jim as we stuff our sleeping bags. "Let's bring this thing down."

About five A.M. we head up our fixed ropes. We leave our bivy gear behind in order to ascend unencumbered. We plan to tag the top and descend back to this ledge in one push.

I ascend the rope first to organize the top anchor. Jim comes up next. I pull up the ropes, and Jim leads a long pitch of intricate stemming and jamming, his hands and feet either wedged into the cracks or bridged off two opposite walls that form a corner. As we gain altitude we can see over the mountain ridge to the west onto the ice cap, where soaring mountains and brilliant white paint the slice of the western horizon that we can see framed by Desmochada and the Northwest Buttress of Poincenot. It's like looking through a giant's magnifying lens. A treasure waits out in that world of ice—I can sense it—and someday I hope to have the moxie to try to find it.

Jim gets his hero lead next—100 feet up a strenuous squeeze chimney. My belay is a comfortable seat of yellow granite. Protection is sparse, but the rope runs out steadily through my hands. Jim may be built like an underfed coyote, but he has a lion's heart, and he manages to look almost graceful as he wiggles his way up the bold squeeze, an old school Yosemite-style lead that would reduce most modern hot-shots to grovels and snivels.

A series of grunts come down the crack, and I take that as my cue to go up second. I arrive at Jim's footrail stance above the chimney. "Righteous lead."

"Look," answers Jim, "we're way above the ledge we bivied on in that storm." Down and to the right it looks minuscule.

Two pitches of stunning crack climbing come my way. I jam hands and fists while sweeps of granite fall away beneath my feet. Well over a thousand feet below, the granite meets slopes of snow and ice in the little pocket valley. With every glance to the right I see the ice cap behind the Torres. Each move up, each obstacle surpassed, yields a new section of stone whose problems must be solved. We have no certain knowledge that the crack systems we are following go all the way to the summit ridge or if they are even possible for climbers of our ability and with our small supply of hardware to climb, but such is the curse, blessing, and the satisfaction of being first.

Above, Jim deals with two more fine pitches of chimneying. He avoids both cruxes with elegant moves on flakes of stone to the left of the chimney.

Then it's my turn to lead and I go up. I dodge an overhang, and the crack I'm climbing narrows to two inches, then steepens and narrows to an inch. Then the crack necks down to a barely open seam. I slot our most minute camming device into the seam, clip the rope through the attached carabiner, and call "tension" to Jim. He reels the slack in through his belay plate, takes the rope tight, and I dangle just below the cam. Above, the seam disappears into a monolithic sweep of smooth, crackless, holdless stone. There is no way to continue above without drilling holes and placing bolts, and since Jim and I didn't bring a bolt kit and would be loath to use it even if we had, I crane my neck around and look for other options.

I need to find another crack. Until now this route of discovery up 1,500 feet of coarse Patagonian granite has been the first ascent I have always dreamed of making, but if I can't get to another crack, our route won't "go," and our efforts of the last two days (and the last week) will go to waste. I suspiciously examine the top cam, which supports all my weight, to make sure it's totally solid and yell for Jim, unseen fifty feet below, beneath the overhang, to "lower me." Five feet, ten feet, fifteen feet, and "Hold!" To my left there is nothing but blank granite, but to my right there is hope—a corner that faces away from me. I can't quite see into the back of the corner, but there are often cracks in such features. And the corner looks as if it connects to an arching crack above.

If I can swing over into the corner, if the corner holds a crack, and if I can climb it, we'll be able to continue our ascent.

I swing over. The pendulum is easy, and it doesn't take much effort to get a look into the shallow corner.

I hang in stunned silence and stare into the maw of a five-inch crack, the worst possible size. Five inches is too big to hold our biggest piece of protection (a #4 Camalot) and too small to admit my whole body. This universally feared crack size, known as "offwidth," is too big for fist jams and too small to climb chimney-style. It's a crack size that climbers shun like venereal disease. I have two options—tackle this sixty-foot section of offwidth or go down in defeat.

Jim senses my hesitation, even from below, where he can't see, and calls up, "What's it like?"

"Grim. It's a five-inch medal-of-honor crack. I don't know if I can do it."

Jim doesn't answer.

I dangle and ponder the last days of alpine struggle. The summit is within striking distance, and it takes so much to get here.

If I go for it, fall, and get hurt, say break a bone or two, Jim and I are days from a hospital, and that assumes Jim could get me down alone. There is no expectation of rescue here in Patagonia. Jim could leave me here and descend to get help, but there would be no point. There's no helicopter rescue service to call, and even if there was, by the time Jim got down and organized an airlift, a storm would almost certainly wrap the peaks and no chopper could brave such weather. Doug Byerly and Rolando Garibotti are the only two people who even know what mountain Jim and I are on, and right now they're totally committed to their own adventure on the north side of Fitzroy. We are 100 percent on our own. My fear wells up.

Knowing when to say "no" is a cornerstone of good alpine judgment, the kind of judgment that keeps climbers alive. No one, least of all Jim, would reproach me for deciding to bag it. Jim and I once climbed four decent pitches up a new route in Alaska, then discovered that neither of us was getting a good vibe from the climb; something just wasn't right. We couldn't summon a single concrete reason to quit, but neither of us could shake the ominous feeling, and so we made a completely intuitive decision to bail out. We didn't return for another attempt, and I have no regret about the new route that got away.

This is a real and fascinating paradox of alpinism: You must care completely, and at the same time you can't care at all. You must give yourself over to the she-wolf of desire and strive toward success and the summit with every ounce of strength, every iota of commitment, every fiber of being. But at exactly the same time that you climb with the full power of desire, you must be able to judge the evolving situation as uncontrollable and abandon ascent without hesitation. It's too easy to die up here.

I hang on the cusp of a dream. We've already had to swallow one failure, and I don't want to choke down another. For more than a decade I've dreamed about doing a first ascent of such magnitude and quality. Since boyhood I've fantasized about an adventure like this. There is such intense satisfaction in seeing this wild part of the planet with the first set of human eyes and touching it with the first set of human hands. I look up at the crack closely. Can I do this? I simply cannot fall. I take a few deep breaths in an effort to make an unemotional decision. Confidence is essential in the alpine game, but it must not lead to hubris. We've been so busy engineering the danger and uncertainty out of the world that we humans rarely get opportunities to perform deliberate acts of physical courage.

Goddamnit, yes, I can do this. Goddamnit, I want to do this, and I run myself up into the breach. In no way is Poincenot's summit assured, but if we fail, then I'm going to fail at full bore.

"Hang on, Jim, I'm going for it."

I cuss my way up the crack, sweating with fear. Beyond the first few feet of progress I must continue up—to down climb this horrible slot is unthinkable.

Thirty feet up I get two solid pieces of gear under a flake on the right side of the slot and allow myself to contemplate survival. Thirty more feet and I struggle up the last five-inch section to where the crack widens enough to permit my entire body inside. Chimneying, normally unpleasant and awkward, never felt so good, because once inside the chimney there's little chance that I'll fall. I struggle up behind a huge block wedged across the chimney. After this caving maneuver I build an anchor above the chockstone, tie the rope to it, and call down to Jim. I stand atop the block, hook a wrist though the anchor, and ride a celestial adrenaline shot.

I eye the route ahead. Thin cracks go up a steep corner and disappear into what looks like the lower angled slopes of Poincenot's summit ridge. We are close! Jim's weight pulls the rope tight as he comes up the fixed rope.

A cold gust of wind grabs my attention. Lost in ascent, I've neglected to eye the weather. A glance at the ice cap turns my liver to jelly. Gray clouds pile up to the west and swarm toward us. Saucer-shaped lenticular clouds that indicate high winds and moisture cap the Torres and the other peaks of the Andes. A dose of fear squelches my surge.

The view to the ice cap is of heart-stopping beauty, beauty that is almost the polar opposite of the fear caused by the storm boiling up beyond. I stand on the chockstone, wait for Jim, and try to maintain my balance between those two poles—beauty like a siren song that draws me only forward and fear that drives me back. I've been trying to hold that balance for more than a week, and it takes a constant strain of will.

Jim wedges himself up through the rock tunnel and steps onto the top of the chockstone. "We've got to hurry if we're gonna beat this storm."

I hastily reorganize the rack of protection and score a beautiful thin crack lead above, then Jim leads the last pitch of hand crack to the summit ridge while I belay. The wind is formidable, and a layer of gray rockets east some hundred yards over our heads. Psychologically, the time spent belaying can be difficult. There's plenty of time to think. Under nonextreme circumstances I enjoy the downtime tremendously—I kick it on a ledge, deal the string in or out while my pal climbs. I keep a part of my mind alert to his or her situation, but another part is free to roam. But here, now, I'm anxious and fidgety and there's no joy in the idleness, since I can't stop my mind from contemplating the fury of the oncoming storm.

I go up to join Jim at his stance on the summit ridge. "Okay, Greg, let's stash most of the gear and the second rope here. We'll just cruise up, tag the summit, and get the hell out of here." I agree. The summit can't be more than a few hundred feet to our left. Three hours remain until dark.

Ice chokes most of the cracks on the summit slopes. Our boots and crampons would be useful, but they're in a waterproof bag we left at the very bottom of the North Face, left there to save weight. We have to deal with the ice in smooth-soled rock shoes, great for ascending rock, but on ice it feels like we've got banana peels tied to our feet. Even the simplest moves are slippery, and we want to hurry so badly. We move gingerly, but as fast as prudence will allow.

All our hopes are pinned on the high point in front of us. We traverse across and worm up an icy chimney to the top of the rock tower, and from atop the tower we see the real summit beyond, at least another hour away. More mountain—and more fear, more doubt, more difficulties, more stress, more risk—looms. The false summit is a crushing blow. I want to cry, to vomit, and I swear with all the venom I can summon. Patagonia, with its perfect form, isn't home to many false summits, isn't usually cunning in its camouflage of the goal, but Poincenot has deceived us because we came at it from an unusual angle. My weak mind automatically concocts an excuse, a story to explain our failure to get to the top.

Angered, I decide the opposite. "Fuck it, Jim, we're rappelling all night, because we are going to stand on top of this Patagonian pile of shit. I'll go back and get the second rope and the gear." I am afraid of the consequences of this unexpected jump in commitment—the all-night descent through darkness and storm—and I say so.

"No big deal," says Jim. "How many times have you done that before? We're gonna be fine. You are the descent king."

Clouds tear all around. I look to the southwest: Walls of black cloud swallow entire mountain ranges. Unroped, I go back for the extra gear. It's easy terrain, but if I slip on the ice or break a hand- or foothold I will die, and the wind has me under pressure to hurry. It costs forty minutes of wasted time to go back and forth over terrain we've already covered in what feels to be the face of impending doom.

Through a long gap in the clouds I can see past the ice cap to snow-capped mountains in the archipelago beyond the ice field. A dark patch below those snow peaks might be ocean water in one of the Pacific's fjords.

With the extra equipment, we fix one rope and rappel down it onto an icy shelf in the cleft between the rock tower and the real summit. We leave it in place and use the second rope to secure our ascent to the summit. Forty minutes of scrambling over ice- and snow-covered rocks later, and I'm belaying on a ledge a few feet below the top. The sun is gone. Clouds whip over our heads.

"Your summit, Jim." He disappears out of view, hollers, and belays me up to join him. We briefly touch gloved hands atop Aguja Poince-not, no words necessary, and take a look around. The plains to the east have already fallen into night, but here among the summits we still have light to see.

The summit is five feet wide and twenty-five feet long and surrounded by monumental drops. Eerie light slips between the cloud layers out on the ice cap beyond the Torres. The lenticulars piled up to the west glow faint orange. Cold gusts batter us. The stone bulk of Fitzroy looms close. Other than the orange lenticulars, the entire world is shades of gray. The ice cap is gray under the clouds. Gray cloud wraps the summit of Fitzroy. To the southeast, the waters of Lago Viedma gleam battleship gray. To the east stretch the lonely deserts of Patagonia, black-gray in gathering darkness. Nine thousand feet below, miles distant, and worlds away, the lone light of an *estancia* on the shores of Lago Viedma twinkles out a greeting from the rest of the human race.

Wind rips at my storm jacket. The world teeters on the brink of Armageddon. Out in the ice cap, a wall of dark cloud swallows another mountain. The view calls to mind some of the words from Tennyson's poem "Ulysses," my favorite, and I fire them off to Jim: ". . . for my purpose holds/To sail beyond the sunset, and the baths/ Of all the western stars, until I die."

"You are so full of shit," he says and laughs in my face.

In times past, Magellan, Drake, and Darwin all battled terrible difficulties to explore parts of Patagonia, and now this small, hitherto unknown part has revealed itself to our endeavors. What a thrill it is to travel in the same vein. But there is no glow of success to enjoy here on this summit. I won't relax and enjoy our ascent until we're sipping whiskey in a Chaltén bar. We've still got to get down, and in Patagonia with a storm coming on, that is a bodacious obstacle.

We spend less than two minutes on top.

Darkness overtakes us before we make it back to the point where our route of ascent met the summit ridge. With headlamps casting small pools of light we rig anchors and rappel into blackness. Miraculously, the ominous clouds don't coalesce into storm, and the agony I have considered so certain doesn't materialize. The wind drops at about one A.M., right when I'm on my knees begging the ropes not to stick as we pull them over the five-inch crack. It's big trouble if they stick above us in that evil slot—I'm sure I can't reclimb it in the dark to free a stuck rope. I nearly weep with relief when the ropes fall cleanly.

However, the rappel above the five-inch slot and the rappel below it both hang up the falling ropes. Jim and I reclimb parts of those pitches to recover the stuck string. Massive clusters, twists, strenuous pulls: There is some new hassle on every rappel.

There are at least two other established descent routes from

Poincenot's summit with anchors already constructed, but neither line would take us back to the ledge where we left our bivy gear. Regardless, I can't possibly handle the anxiety of route finding down unfamiliar terrain in the dark. It's much less mentally taxing to go down the same way that we came up, over familiar terrain, and to execute the descent plan made during the ascent. I've stomached so much fear in the last week that I'll do anything to keep it down, even if it does cost us hundreds of dollars' worth of hardware that we have to leave behind to anchor our rappels.

Just after first light we make it to the broad ledge where we left our sleeping bags, and after a few hours of rest, we continue down to high camp with the last of our strength. Jim and I fall apart in camp, now that the pressure's off, each of us in a separate personal fog. Our alpine binge is over. Four or five times I arise from my comatose state and struggle out of the tent, confused. I think and feel nothing as I stagger around camp and stare dumbly at the Torres. The sky is still windless and blue. It occurs to me that we could go bag another one— if we could just stand up.

The next day we lug our gear out of the cirque, our packs much lighter than on the way in—we have no food, we left three-quarters of our hardware to anchor rappels, and we had to cut one of our ropes on the way down. After a night in base camp, we head to town, drink, and soar with warriors' arrogance. A broad river of whiskey flows through Jim, Doug, and myself. Rolo doesn't drink, but he laughs and cavorts right along with us. We have survived the breach, and now we are down, drunk, and ready to pillage.

•

What do we bring back from through the breach? Nothing. Nothing but memories of the most powerful emotions and visions of cold, perfect places; the sound of utter silence; the howl of storm; the crack and thunder of an avalanche; the clatter and whir of rockfall; the sparkle of the stars; the full power of desire; the sweat of effort; and the taste of real fear. We have looked up at a piece of unclimbed mountain and exercised the true human power—we have imagined a future and then made it happen. But after such a set of fantastic summit moments I am left with a haunting doubt. The question tickles away at the base of my spine whenever I run through the litany of my Patagonian experience. Am I worthy of such moments, am I worthy of such astonishing beauty? And the certain, damning answer is no.

O UR SEASON IS IN THE BAG, OUR THIRST FOR alpine action slaked for a time, our recent ascent enough to carry us back to the United States. After our climb the barometric pressure fell through the floor, and a storm now grips the range. A measure of Patagonian time still remains to us, but both Jim and I know not to ask too much of the mountains, and so we turn our eyes to other ventures. Talk of an old trail that links Estancia Madsen, on the far bank of the river opposite Chaltén, to Estancia Maipú, thirty miles to the northeast on the shores of Lago San Martín, piques our interest. On a map, the route looks feasible. We ask advice around Chaltén and get permission from the local landowners. Thirty miles is a long way to walk, but we're fit from a month of slogging heavy alpine loads, and we figure that if we strip our loads to the bare minimum we'll travel fast and easy and enjoy ourselves. We plan to scrounge wood for fuel along the way, so we don't take a stove, just an aluminum teapot, to go with our sleeping gear, empty water bottles, and a portable pantry of bread, cheese, cookies, steaks, and instant coffee.

•

We walk for a day and a half until we emerge from a forest onto a grassy bench above the coastal plain a mile or two from the near shore of Lago San Martín. The grass has yellowed for the summer. We don't know it, but Estancia Maipú is hidden in a fold of earth right below us, and in error we pound an extra four miles to the wrong *estancia,* where we arrive just in time to help four gauchos finish drinking their lunch. The sweet white jug wine tastes awful after such a long walk, but we do our duty as gracious guests, and their totally looped leader drives us back down the bumpy road to Estancia Maipú in a battered orange Ford pickup while he rants away in slurred Spanish that I can't understand. He drops us in front of Estancia Maipú, and we gently tread on sore feet down the dirt driveway to the main buildings.

Wind tosses the tall trees around us, but here on the sheltered lawn, all is calm. A sprinkler waters the grass in the yard, and carefully tended roses grow under lace-curtained windows. I push aside a gate in a waist-high white painted fence and approach the front door. My knock gets no response. We scout up and down the house but detect no one. I return to the front door. It isn't locked and I go inside. The wooden floor of the entryway creaks with age. I walk through an open arch into the dining room and step carefully alongside an elegant table set for twelve. A cozy chair stands in a corner with a brass lamp beside it. The view out the long window beside the table to the lake is magnificent. The room is wide and airy, warm and quiet, while the wind tears through the trees outside. Off the dining room is a hallway lined with empty guest rooms. I feel like I've trespassed in a fairy tale. I've never seen an *estancia* in such perfect condition. This place is Old

World, and immaculate, and shows the pride of a woman's touch. But I can't find her.

Back out front Jim has his shoes and socks off and he's enjoying himself in a dry and sunny patch of grass. I scout the outbuildings and find all the implements for managing a sheep station, but no people. I hear a door slam, investigate, and spot a kitchen attached to the side of the main building.

The woman within is stunned to discover a Spanish-speaking gringo tapping on her window. She lets me in. A 1930s vintage pot-bellied woodstove has the small square kitchen heated to a tropical degree. I peel off my windbreaker and a layer of long underwear until I'm comfortable in a T-shirt. María Ines Leyenda is a happy, fine-looking woman. I arrange for us to spend the night in the *estancia*'s bunkhouse, where she rents beds to travelers not attached to their creature comforts. María Ines asks what we would like for dinner.

I say our tastes are simple, we'd like something typical of the *estancia*. She promises mutton.

María Ines and I sit at a small table in her kitchen wedged between counter and window and talk in simple Spanish. Her grandfather built Estancia Maipú with his own hands in the 1930s. She grew up here, and she now runs the place. The hands are out with the sheep. The smell of good cooking permeates the room. María Ines talks of the glory days of the Patagonian *estancias,* when the price of wool was high, labor cheap, and there was plenty of money. From my seat at the kitchen window I see over a bed of roses and a swath of emerald-green grass to a row of pink and blue lupines and a line of tall, wind-bowed trees planted by the able hand of her grandfather. Past the line of trees the *estancia*'s scrubby pastures rise to meet the rocky slopes of El Nido de los Cóndores, the Condors' Nest, a crag that towers a few thousand feet above Estancia Maipú.

Steep grassy slopes sweep down past the buildings to the frothy waters of Lago San Martín. I am seeing one of the most beautiful Patagonian *estancias,* but the broken terrain also makes La Maipú one of the most difficult *campos* to ranch. Sheep are constantly lost in falls and to pumas raiding the stock from the mountain fastness behind. Although guanacos are plentiful in the high country, they are much more wily and hard to ambush than stupid, slow-moving sheep, and pumas easily acquire a taste for mutton. Dozens of her animals are lost each year, while María Ines's neighbors, who ranch on flat, featureless, and far less attractive terrain farther east, manage a stable flock that thrives without much care. María Ines Leyenda is caught between a ranch that won't cover its expenses and her love for a fading way of life. By way of compromise she has turned her *estancia*'s main buildings into a well-appointed, beautifully landscaped, and spectacularly isolated inn. The nearest store is down a dirt road and nearly a hundred miles away, in the town of Tres Lagos.

After dinner I sit in the grass alongside the bunkhouse while Jim takes advantage of the wood-fired shower inside. I stretch out on my side and prop my head on my elbow in an effort to milk the most warmth from the sun before it sinks into the storm clouds that boil over the mountains to the west. My view rolls out way beyond the far shore of the lake. This vista is so essentially Patagonian—pure as the cold wind, bright as the yellow sun—that it seems to stretch a thousand miles. With it I reflect on our thirty-mile walk over from Chaltén.

•

Jim and I crossed the river opposite Chaltén midmorning, and hiked up the steep slope above Estancia Madsen. Every step took us farther from the new Patagonia of Chaltén's bars, restaurants, and tourists, and closer to the old Patagonia of guanacos, gauchos, *estancias,* thrashing grass, and surging wind. From the slope above Estancia Madsen, we went down through a beech forest to the valley bottom and across the open land of Estancia Canigo. We drank from a clear stream, then climbed a 3,000-foot slope. There wasn't a scrap of vegetation as we crossed the ridge, just rust-colored rocks savaged by the angry wind. I felt as if I were treading on the blasted bones of the earth. Miles behind us the storm wouldn't release Cerro Torre, but the stone bulk of Fitzroy boiled out of the storm and towered among the spreading clouds like Rodin's statue of caped, brooding Balzac. We braced and scrambled through the flying grit over into the lee of the ridge.

Hours later we stood on the nose of a spur and stared down into the bottom of the valley of the Río Portones. Yellow-green grass lined the valley bottom, but there wasn't a single bush, let alone a tree, for as far as our eyes could see. From this vantage we scoped the next ten to fifteen miles of our walk. We wouldn't cover close to that distance this evening, but we matched tomorrow's terrain to the map. Jim led the way down into the valley and we continued upstream alongside the silty waters of the river.

We were excited to see our first guanaco. Ten minutes later we had seen a dozen, and before dark we had seen two hundred. The valley and hillsides teemed with guanaco and echoed with their strange bugle calls. The guanacos traveled in bands of five to ten, each group with their own guide, and they panicked if we appeared on a hillside above them. When they held the high ground and we went by below, they kept their distance but stayed quite relaxed.

Far off over the desert to the east, yellow and pink evening light splashed along the near side of a pile of lenticular clouds stacked like plates high into the atmosphere. There was no wood with which to make a fire. We tossed our packs down into a tiny wash sheltered from the wind and set about scavenging some fuel. I went upstream, Jim went down. I found nothing. In the end I pulled up tufts of dried grass and stripped the thickest roots. The best ones were thinner than string.

Jim returned with a double handful of the same. Jim prepared the cook site while I made another long loop and brought back a few antique cow patties.

Jim raised his eyebrows.

"They work in India, big guy."

We cursed and laughed and seared the meat over a pathetic smoky fire. Fortunately the meat was cut thin, and the twigs and turds cooked up a mean pair of steaks.

Overnight it spotted with rain. At first light, a black-gray wall of cloud crept up the valley toward us. We shook loose from our sleeping bags and laced our shoes. We shouldered our gear, turned our backs to the storm, and marched away without breakfast. For two hours we climbed up between featureless rock-brown hills into a pass. The cloud wall behind us had stalled, but the wind cut out ahead of it like a scythe. The top of the pass was fairly flat, nearly a mile long, and we didn't tread on a single blade of grass as we crossed it. We sheltered down behind a boulder to admire the hidden valley on the far side. Troops of guanacos were spread out on grassy terraces below and condors circled in the waves of wind over our heads. Miles ahead, and thousands of feet lower, were the aquamarine waters of Lago San Martín. The arm of the lake was wide; beyond it rose brown hills.

The wind chased us as we descended steep shale slopes, forded swift streams, crossed green meadows, and squished through bogs. Jim found a fossil swirl the size of a dinner plate on a flat square of rock. Ten semiwild horses eyed us as we dodged down to the trees on the near bank of the Río Elena, where we gathered wood and built a fire for a brunch of steaks and coffee. I lay on my back in a warm patch of sun and listened to the river *shoosh* over rocks and to the wind as it rushed through the trees. The blue sky above us sparkled with the polish of wind.

After the rest we busted straight down the riverbed. The valley walls closed to hem us in. I pulled my pants up over my knees and waded the stream, first one bank, then the other, then we just splashed down the middle of the knee-deep flow. I felt like I did as a boy, exploring "unknown" creeks that often went right through people's backyards, playing at being an explorer, commando, raider, or whatever, always craving to see over the next fallen log, past the next pile of brush, up into the next stagnant, algae-filled pool. That boyhood world was magic, and the fantasies in my mind were as real as the dirt we ground into our clothes. The cold water felt good in my grit-filled shoes, and I knew the magic that pulls me time and again to Patagonia—to explore and climb in Patagonia—childhood magic, when every step was a discovery, charged with meaning, pregnant with possibility. That magic, that fascination, that discovery, that private world shared only with my picked companions—it's all here in Patagonia for me, and the danger, technique, and privations of alpine climbing only serve to whet those childlike sensations to a keen adult edge. I know of no other combination like it and I will return as long as I am able to wrap that Patagonian magic around my heart.

THE LURE OF UNEXPLORED, UNCLIMBED TER-
rain spurred Jim and me twice to Alaska before the same lure
drew me back to Patagonia, but Jim and I weren't able to continue our run together. Jim went off to Antarctica to guide a
wealthy client, a trip I'd love to take but couldn't possibly afford. Jim came back from Antarctica via Patagonia, but we
couldn't make our schedules intersect, and so that's how I
came to find myself taking a pounding at the hands of Aguja
Saint-Exupéry and the Patagonian sky with J. Jay Brooks,
whom I had met in the Alaska Range two years before.

·

Beaten, beaten, and beaten again. White-hot blasts hammer
me against the snow slope. Body and soul I lust for the tent,
pitched under the lee of a shelter stone thousands of feet
below. Only there will we escape this storm. Furiously
driven snow scorches my unprotected eyeballs, my glasses
long since made useless by a frozen crust and stuffed in a
pocket. Blurry, uncorrected vision adds to my isolation. This

slope of frozen snow would be ridiculously easy to descend were it not for angry buffets of wind that assault my balance. We're not using a rope because we're not belaying, and a rope tied between us would only ensure that if one person falls the other one will be yanked off as well.

The gale rages and tries to buffet my axe and crampon points loose from their hold in the névé. The world blasts by in a white-gray fuzz. Mad winds come from random directions: updrafts, downdrafts, and from both sides. J. Jay fights his own battle some sixty-five feet below, his dark form just visible through the gray blasts. The wind cuts us apart; flying snow chunks lash my storm suit with a sound like gravel thrown against a wooden wall. In the acoustic background is the deep toneless growl of the tempest as it blasts through the col over our heads. Communication is impossible. We each struggle down alone.

A rising roar announces another gust. With cold, aching hands I plant the shaft of my axe in the snow, lean into the slope, and clutch the axe head to steady myself. I stand firmly planted against the gust, which pelts over me and disappears with a *whoosh* between the spires above. Patagonia hates me.

I continue down the snow slope behind J. Jay. A few hundred feet farther down we traverse off the snow slope and scramble down a series of rocky steps and take a quick breather in the lee of a big granite boulder. None of the summits over our heads are visible through the winging gray. We're suspended in a sea of angry gray shades—the clouds are gray, the snow is gray, the stone is gray.

"Two hours till a hot brew."

We exchange other such motivational platitudes before we continue the march down and across a series of snowfields, talus slopes, ravines, and rock shelves, most made slick by a dusting of new snow that sits over a thin layer of verglass. The storm batters us at every step.

During the last hour of descent we fixate on a tiny green dot that sits far below us in the sea of gray stone that constitutes the immense lateral moraine of the Torre Glacier. I'm on autopilot, but that green dot grows as we descend until I can see it wobble back and forth in blasts of wind. Taut ripples race over the green nylon fabric of the tent as it tugs at the lines with which we've guyed it to braced blocks of granite. It's a relief to find our high-camp tent intact with the storm at full power.

A few minutes later I'm cast ashore inside the tent, bathed in the gray-green light that filters through the nylon, lying inert underneath my sleeping bag while J. Jay lies inert under his. Neither of us says much; even my thoughts are mired in the mud of physical exhaustion. The tent flaps and snaps in the local gusts, and the flood of wind through the peaks above makes exactly the sound that rises to the lip of a deep canyon as a river roars through rapids far below. Time passes. Beaten again, thwarted by the great wild flood of the Patagonian west wind.

I fiddle with the stove, spark it to life, and heat water. We gulp down big swallows of hot chocolate and chase them with a cup full of instant mashed potatoes seasoned with butter, salt, and precious drops of Tabasco sauce. We snooze and stretch and hang damp gloves and socks from lengths of thin parachute cord tied across the top of the tent. Lunch is crackers, cheese, and cups of tea. We each munch a Snickers bar for dessert, then carefully twist the top from the water bottle into which we decanted a bottle of cheap Argentine whiskey before making the trek up from base camp. The slugs go down like turpentine, but they dull our pain. I wouldn't taste this rot at gunpoint back home, but in this range, in this storm, in this tent, this whiskey is priceless.

The snorts of whiskey lead us into another snooze. We wake hours later, with just enough time before dark to cook up a meal of buttered noodles and tuna sprinkled with grated cheese and generous dabs of

Tabasco sauce. We shovel it down. J. Jay quickly falls back to sleep after dinner, but I can't, and for half the night I lie awake in blackness and follow the rise and fall of the local gusts backed by the sepulchral moan of the wind that drives the storm through the night sky. The worst thing that could happen while we're in this state is that the weather could improve.

Happily, it doesn't. After coffee and breakfast, J. Jay plows into the heart of *War and Peace;* I lie with my back propped against my boots and spare clothes and alternately write in a gray notebook and stare at the foot of the tent. Sometime before noon I clamber out of the tent onto the gravel plateau. The storm churns off the ice cap and wraps the upper halves of the three Torres. I glimpse the Col of Conquest between Cerro Torre and Torre Egger, beneath the cloud bank that stretches off the Torres and reaches across the deep valley to touch the tops of Fitzroy and Poincenot, where tongues of cloud flicker and swirl from both summits. The sun hangs fuzzy between those summits. Irregular and infrequent dapples of sunshine dash across our high-camp plateau, often at the same time that rain squalls pelt it. The locomotive growl of the wind that goes over the peaks and through the cols of the Fitzroy massif reaches down to me where I stand seven or eight thousand feet below, the voices of the angry gods whose whims thwart my ambitions.

The wind assaults me. It takes effort to maintain my feet. Rain squalls pelt the tent, wind dashes through the great valley and streams toward the steppes, lusting for the Atlantic and the freedom to circle the globe once more. Up here in the Torre Cirque, perched on this small plateau between Fitzroy and Cerro Torre and their spectacular satellites while a storm pounds across the Andes, our isolation is complete. Although the world of rustic restaurants, telephone cabins, fax machines, youth hostels, and small grocery stores is but fifteen miles away, there is no help for us souls lost in this cirque of great mountains, mighty glaciers, and angry southern sky. J. Jay and I haven't seen another human being in five or six days, since before our last aborted attempt, and with the weather so foul we're not likely to either.

Patagonia grates: Strenuous carries and multiple attempts wear on our bodies, uncertainties assail our psyches. Is tomorrow the day? Do these gentle evening breezes herald a midnight screamer? Should we go for it? Will we get another chance? Is our route viable? Does it "go"? How will we get down if a storm catches us up high? All of these questions are real, and I don't have the answer to a single one. Even the damned wind is a constant uncertainty. I hear a gust approach, my tension rises, I brace, but impact doesn't come as the gust races down a neighboring ravine or through an adjacent pile of boulders. Another gust rushes close but misses. The edges of the next catch me slightly, just enough to ruffle my jacket. The fourth blasts me square in the chest and shakes the tent with unconcealed gusto. The wind unzips the tent flaps, rips a jacket out of a hand, grabs a hat off a head, lashes the eyes with the loose straps of a backpack, sprouts holes in the walls of the tent where it touches a rock. The only certainty is that if a storm catches us in action it'll hurl every weapon in the arsenal: wind, rain, snow, sleet, cold, hunger, thirst, exhaustion, torn and swollen hands, and big, big fear. J. Jay thinks the Patagonian weather is mischievous; I think it's downright malignant, but it's worth coming so far if only to watch the sky and feel the wind. We are insignificant motes of life, two alien creatures in a hostile landscape of icy stone and split screaming sky.

It's impossible not to like J. Jay Brooks, a redhead with a gymnast's frame, a quick smile, and laughing eyes. When most people say, "I thought I was gonna die," it's a cliché. If J. Jay says it, you believe him. Two and a half years ago on a mountainside in Alaska, a huge rockfall crushed J. Jay's shoulder to dust and cut the ropes. J. Jay's partner was stranded with two short pieces of rope 180 feet above. J. Jay had two almost full-length ropes, but he was nearly a thousand feet above the glacier and spurting blood. J. Jay couldn't afford to go into shock, and he couldn't afford to wait. If he quit or lost concentration he would die. Awash in blood, he rigged rappels and rescued himself. Below the climb he staggered across the glacier to their camp in a daze, spattering blood on the snow in a trail a yard wide. Luckily, J. Jay fell into the hands of two other climbers, and they organized his evacuation and then plucked his stranded partner off the wall. When Jim and I visited J. Jay in an Anchorage hospital a week later, he was waxy white, he wasn't conscious, and he had already had several of his many surgeries. Since the accident, J. Jay has worked as a high-profile commercial mortgage broker, and he travels all the time, but he has to carry an X ray in order to get on airplanes—otherwise, the mass of metal in his revamped shoulder lights up metal detectors and security won't let him through. Modern medicine returned some use of his shoulder. That he is again climbing a hard mountain is due to the unflagging commitment with which he painfully rehabilitated himself.

Some days later we run out of food and hike the miles down the glacier to base camp. The Río Fitzroy burbles and runs past camp in recently unfrozen freedom, the waters rushing toward the distant sea. The late-summer evening stretches into night, and I sit in a hut and share boxes of wine with J. Jay and Charlie Fowler. I've seen Charlie only twice, at outdoor-industry trade shows, since we shared that sublime sunrise on Cerro Torre's summit. Since then Charlie has relentlessly explored mountains in China, Tibet, and other parts of Central Asia. The man's life is a string of mountain expeditions, often planned two or three in advance, with short vacations in between at home in Norwood, Colorado.

But the last time Charlie went to Asia, eighteen months ago, the expedition didn't end happily. Charlie was in western Tibet with two friends, all roped together and descending from the summit of a

25,000-foot mountain. One man fell, and pulled Charlie and the other man after him. They fell 5,000 feet, bashing down an icy slope, and at the bottom pitched over a 300-foot ice cliff. Miraculously, nobody died in the fall, although everybody was bashed up. Charlie hurt his leg; he thought it was broken. Crawling, it took them three days to get down to their base camp. It took Charlie four more days to get to a hospital. Charlie's fingers and toes were frostbitten. His fingers recovered; his toes did not. He had to have three of them cut completely off, and he lost parts of two others. The knee injury and the loss of his toes slowed him down for most of a year, and Charlie missed last season in Patagonia, but he's back this year, albeit wearing smaller shoes.

I perch on one of the hut's wooden benches with a blue plastic bucket clutched between my knees, and use the pliers of a Leatherman tool to push the tip of a nail into the plastic rim of the bucket. I push in another nail two inches from the first. Lauchas, a type of virulent rat-mouse that lives in Patagonia, have in recent nights ravaged the chow that we have stashed in the little hut, and as Charlie, J. Jay, and I sip wine and the light fades, we refine the construction of a mousetrap we've used in years past to massacre a horde of the little beasts.

I rotate the bucket 180 degrees and poke two more nails into the rim directly across from the first pair, put the bucket in the dirt between my feet, and balance a section of a broken trekking pole across the top of the bucket between the improvised nail brackets. I give the pole a test spin, and it whirls freely.

"Find me something stinky," I say, and Charlie opens a can of greasy sardines, irresistible to any rodent brigand. I pinch up a choice morsel of the slimy fish, and rub it around the middle of the ski pole. I suck my fingers clean and Charlie passes me a water bottle so I can rinse my hand and fill the bucket halfway.

I wiggle out a slat of wood that's tucked behind my bench, break it down to three feet with the sole of my shoe, and use it to create a bridge between the rim of the bucket and the dirt bank at the back of the hut.

If the trap functions properly, a laucha will smell the irresistible sardine bait and march to the bucket's rim across the slat bridge. He'll hesitate, aware of the water in the bucket. But no self-respecting scavenger can resist a free meal, and he'll reach forward with a single paw. He can perhaps touch the sardine-slathered ski pole, but not quite get his snout into the feast. He'll bring his second forefoot forward in a fatal attempt to brace himself on the ski pole. Lauchas are nimble, but they're not gymnasts, and with half his weight committed to the spinning pole and his little claws unable to get purchase on the metal, the pole will rotate and pitch the unbalanced beast into the bucket of water. The poor little bastard can tread water, but not forever, and he'll drown there in the bottom of the bucket. The true beauty of the device is that whatever orientation the pole takes once it has spun off its first victim, the trap remains armed, ready for another, and they march to their watery end by the battalion.

We discuss various refinements to the lethal contraption. I suggest that we lubricate the spinning ends of the ski pole with cooking oil in order to smooth its action. Charlie and J. Jay nix my idea, worried that the lauchas might be pulled off the sardine scent by distracting food odors. With a few more swallows of the dollar-a-liter wine, Charlie, J. Jay, and I envision a parade of Patagonian climbers marching along the slat, each one eagerly groping toward a summit at the valley's head before they plummet to their doom. We snort and chuckle and talk our way onto other subjects.

It's long been dark outside, and the corner has long since been torn from the top of the second box of wine when Charlie abruptly announces, after hours of conversation, "Hey, today's my birthday."

We're shocked. "Jesus Christ, Charlie, why didn't you say anything?"

"I just did."

We raise our cups and toast him. It's February 18, 1999, and Charlie Fowler is forty-five years old. He has been an avid climber for thirty-one years, ever since he was a freshman in high school, and he has perhaps seen more mountain terrain in South America and Central Asia than any man since Sir Eric Shipton.

Charlie drains his wine and opts for bed; J. Jay follows suit. I stay alone and nurse my last sips while I stare at a candle's steady flame. Yellow-orange light casts dark dancing shadows behind the bags and jars of food that line the walls of the decaying hut. I listen to the river murmur and to the whoosh of the wind. Time passes slowly, but happily.

Come morning I unceremoniously hurl the contents of the bucket into the river. Three dark shapes are in the fan of water that arcs out into midstream.

Big sad drops of rain fall from a steel-gray sky, the wind blows, and the storm drags on for days. During the week that we were at high camp in the cirque, the first colors of autumn tinted some of the leaves on the beech trees that carpet the foothills and valleys around base camp. We slosh to Chaltén and back on a food resupply run. One evening the wind stops and the clouds fade from the sky. We opt to sleep for a few hours, get up at two A.M., and then head up-valley for another attempt, so we load our backpacks and settle into our bags before daylight fades. But I thrash and turn, sleep won't come, and to complete my frustration, J. Jay snores beside me.

I slide out of my sleeping bag, pull on pants and shoes, grab J. Jay's down jacket, quietly unzip the tent flap, and slip out for a walk. Apart from the river's constant soothing rush, the night is absolutely silent. Bright moonlight lances down through the branches and leaves over camp. I weave through the trees and tents and wander out into the treeless boulder field beyond. The full moon floats across the southern sky at its biggest and brightest, and the night has the glossy sheen of rubbed black velvet. Only about a dozen stars show through the moonlight. Mountains stand to the left and right of base camp, while straight up the valley Cerro Torre rises dark and silver into the night, tall and proud like a god. I thread between boulders and find a path that climbs the terminal moraine at the bottom end of Laguna Torre. I tread lightly, but gravel crunches under my feet. Patagonia holds its breath; not a breeze ruffles the lake. Bright as it is, the moon sheds not one iota of warmth, and the cold penetrates.

The moon reflects perfectly from the undistorted black waters of the lake. Square-topped El Mocho sits faithfully to the bottom right of Cerro Torre, while Cerro Torre, Torre Egger, and Cerro Standhardt seem close and rise like titanic fingers above the silver tongue of the massive glacier that drains into the far end of the lake. The mountains and the glacier seem to float above the dark waters. There is no depth perception in this ethereal darkness. The cold numbs my nose and cheeks and penetrates my legs. I sit back against a boulder and wrap my legs one over the other.

With a chilling crack a chunk of ice cleaves off the tongue of the glacier and thunders into the lake, the awful toll of alpine doom like the roar of a lion, a sound that tells what it was like to be human and afraid when the world was young. The echo fades, waves and ripples chase each other across the surface of the lake, and the reflected moon fractures into a palette of hammered silver. My cheeks and neck tingle, and the jolt of fear reverberates down to my fingertips.

•

Exactly twenty-four hours later the wind claws at the Gore-Tex fabric of my bivy sack. In the blackness inside the bag I can see nothing without my headlamp. I wear every stitch of clothing I have. My butt is perched on a coiled rope; my back leans against my nearly empty backpack propped between me and the cold granite. Both are improvised insulation. My legs dangle over the drop, and I prop the heels of my boots on a three-inch ledge below. The bivy sack is zipped shut except for a two-inch airhole in front of my nose. My end of the rope runs from my harness out through the airhole to where it is knotted to a nest of gear that anchors me to this ledge. Here, on a ledge high on the West Face of Aguja Saint-Exupéry, I don't dare untie. The wind snaps and cracks and grabs at the Gore-Tex. I bang my knees together and ram my hands between my thighs in a mostly useless effort to generate warmth.

J. Jay sits and shivers on a similar but separate perch a few feet to my left. There is a lull between the blasts of wind. A knot loosens in my stomach with the absence of noise. The lull lasts just long enough for both of us to feel a surge of hope.

"Maybe this'll just be an overnight blow," I venture from inside the icy depths of my bivy sack, a hope that the rising roar of the returning storm can't quite extinguish. A wild, arrhythmic drum roll thumps over my bivy sack.

Failure, our coming rappel descent, another epic: my old Patagonian friends. Hope is about the only weapon we have left, and we don't have much of that. J. Jay is out of time and must return to his job in a few days. These perches aren't even good enough for us to smash together for warmth. I would love to complete this first ascent on Aguja Saint-Exupéry, a peak named for the French aviator who pioneered airmail routes in Africa and Patagonia and who wrote *Wind, Sand and Stars,* one of my favorite books. Yesterday we climbed about 1,200 feet of virgin stone; perhaps another thousand still stand above us.

Later, made claustrophobic by the stale air trapped inside the bivy sack, I cuss and thrash my head out through the zipper and into the fresh frigid air of the night. The wind still runs at full bore, but the cold air on my face drives away the panic of confinement. I twist on my perch and watch the moon where it sits on the shoulder of Aguja Saint-

Exupéry. The upper reaches of this mountain are dark and jagged against the gray-black sky and the white orb of the moon. Across the valley to the west, dull moonlight gleams from the leading edge of the clouds that boil off the ice cap and roll over the three Torres. Only the black base of each peak is visible beneath the clouds of tarnished silver. Ghostly thin clouds cut free from the ice cap and race over the valley to flee across the face of the moon. The great white glacier streaked with black rock flows through the valley below. Gusts of wind come on like a flood.

J. Jay sits and shivers with his thoughts; I sit and shiver with mine. We'll try to push on in the morning if the storm presents the slightest opportunity, but it'll be the defiant act of stubborn fools in the face of meteorologic fact and inevitable defeat. We are beaten; I can feel it in my bones. This storm is not going to break, there is going to be no fourth opportunity to complete this route we've been trying to force up the Southwest Face of Aguja Saint-Exupéry. This year there will be no clean buzz of success to carry me home to the sunny winter skies of California. This year I will take home only questions. The upper third of our route remains to be solved. Will another team one day unthread the mountain's intricacies? Will our future yield another trip, another attempt, another opportunity? Or only more failure? Hell, why am I even thinking about the future? The future is irrelevant—a tough descent still divides us from the day after tomorrow.

The fact that I will return home having failed to do what I set out to accomplish is a particularly repugnant dish to choke down. I shiver, and ponder different tactics and equipment that we might have employed, different preparations. Preparation, opportunity, and experience are the cornerstones of alpine success, and you cannot get by on the last one alone. We have worked hard, climbed well, and suffered. We have done nothing seriously wrong, and still we're not going to stand on the summit of Saint-Exupéry.

Success and failure dog all people. But if success is measured by routes completed and summits trodden, most of us alpinists fail far more often than we succeed. A long string of failure can eat at the inside of a man like a hemorrhagic fever. Even your best friends are apt to see your trips only in terms of summits achieved. Imagine how terrible it is to invest thousands of hard-won dollars and months of life only to come home to explain failure. That "it was a great experience even if we didn't climb it" business is a hard sell. There isn't much success in "I tried." It's hard to find success in repeated failure, and harder still to explain it. Many times I've done everything right, busted my ass and risked it in exactly the right dosages, only to be hammered by storm with my neck far into the alpine noose. Whether or not we get to stand on top often depends on forces far out of our hands. But to fail well, that is our prerogative, and our pride.

"All I want," says superhardman Rolando Garibotti, by far the best of us climbing in Patagonia the day that J. Jay and I were on Saint-Exupéry, "is to fight the good fight." Jim Donini stands as tall on the strength of his failures as he does on his successes. He failed to do the first ascent of Cerro Standhardt, he failed in China, he failed with me on Cerro Torre's Compressor Route, he failed in Peru, he failed on Latok I's North Ridge and on Baintha Brakk in Pakistan. He sports myriad Alaskan failures. But he failed magnificently. The only real alpine failure is the collapse of will, and I can't imagine Donini ever suffering that collapse. Success is to endure, to persevere, to act in the face of real fear and opportunity. Success is to chart your own seas and steer for a personal star.

Statistics tell the true story of Patagonian failure. Half of the attempts make the long slog to the base of the objective mountain and perhaps make a few rope lengths of progress before being abandoned in the face of obviously deteriorating weather. Much energy is spent, but it's easy to get down. During another quarter of the attempts the

good weather lasts long enough for us to get high on a mountain before the weather turns. The storms then catch us far from safety and
we have to fight for our lives. The final quarter of the time we end on
top. Someday soon we'll have accurate weather forecasts at our disposal in Patagonia, but I don't look forward to that event. I like things
the way they are. Doubt is the most essential ingredient in the alpine
emotional stew. The denouement of each attempt is unknown, and
even if three-quarters of the time hearts are laid open for nothing,
there is no future in pessimism, and so I aspire to shoulder the load and
head uphill, every time.

Alpinists fail all over the world, but Patagonia is the true alpine
Verdun, where wars of attrition seldom pay summit dividends. But
like most of my peers, I've never shouldered a pack and headed up
without being sure that this time, *this time,* we're going to the top. As I
approach the base of a peak, the thought catches me: "After we do this,
what can we do next?" And I indulge in a flying fantasy that after we do
this mountain we'll go do that one, and then that one.

It has never played out that way . . . not yet.

I respect failure—Patagonia has made it so. Anybody who makes it
in a tough field can rightly pour scorn on people who run their mouths
off without making the necessary commitment or doing the hard work
success demands. But people who pursue big dreams with their whole
hearts deserve big-league respect even if they come up short. Much of
success is earned with bloody hard work, but certain individuals are
blessed with talent, and blind luck also spices every single success, regardless of talent, and, anyway, a person probably has the gap between
his performance and his potential closed to the smallest that it's ever
going to be in those few moments right before success.

Why climb, especially in Patagonia, given such failure? As I said in
the opening chapter, there is no sentence, no paragraph that will explain why. *Why* refuses distillation. Consider those two classic alpine

saws: "Because it's there" and "If you've got to ask you ain't ever gonna know." Both strike me as true, but inadequate. And then my favorite, courtesy of Donini: "Because it's the only thing I've ever been any good at." Great sound bites, yes, but whole truth does not jump out of a sound bite. Such quips are also dismissals.

Perhaps the best answer is: because I love it. I love it even as I am freezing my ass on this cold, dark bivy high on the walls of Aguja Saint-Exupéry. I love everything about it without qualification. I love to coil ropes and to carry heavy loads. I love the sky and I love the storm, the ice, and the stone. I love to succeed and I love to try. I love to wait and I love to act; I love to shiver and I love to sweat. I love the freedom and I love the discipline. I love Patagonia, and I love to climb.

Perhaps the worst answer is: because it is an escape. Patagonia is an engagement, not an escape. It eliminates distraction and provides an opportunity to close that gap between my potential and my performance. The goal of the mind might be to survive and reach the summit, but behind that goal lies a more elusive objective, one perhaps better described as a hope. And that hope carries me time and again to the mountains of Patagonia, for I hope that the mountains of Patagonia make me a better man.

A little light seeps into the bivy sack.

"J. Jay, it's getting light. Time to get hot." Time to get on with the business of failure.

•

The wind howls, screams, whirls, pummels: My world is no larger than what exists inside my thin shell of storm clothing supplemented with what little information my senses can gather from the world outside. My glasses froze into uselessness last night, so I'm left with my imperfect vision further blurred by gray belts of cloud and snow. The hood of my storm jacket and the lip of my helmet cut off my peripheral vision. I hear little besides the loud snaps of my clothing and the mad howl of the wind as it careens through the range. J. Jay and I are shoulder to shoulder on a tiny ledge, but we can communicate only with shouts and wild gestures. Everything else is lost in the drowning din of storm. We've come down about 400 feet, with 800 crucial feet to go before the snow slope and the slog down to high camp. I am hungry and damn thirsty. Numb hands and feet dull my sense of touch. My cheeks are white-cold. Snow pellets whip into my face and scorch my eyeballs. I can only squint against a raised glove in this flying madness. It takes all my attention and all my concentration to execute the simple tasks essential to retreat. There is no past, and until we can reach safe ground far below there is no future. Life is just this torturous present. There is much to fear, but right now, stuck in pure action frightfully distilled, I feel as if I could shoulder the sky.

I ram the free ends of the ropes into my empty backpack, which dangles from the front of my waist harness. J. Jay wrestles the heavy pack and lends what help he can. I will go down first with the hardware and a lighter load to fiddle with the ropes and build the next set of anchors 180 feet below. Both ropes are joined with a knot and clipped to a carabiner we've sacrificed to the anchor in front of us; the slack ends of the ropes are stuffed in the backpack to stop the storm from hopelessly tangling them. The wind swats us from side to side, swaying us in unison like puppets.

Check, check, and double-check—an old Army aphorism, and a bloody useful one considering that a dumb mistake made by numb hands in fumbling gloves will kill us. The brown granite in front of me and the anchor I recently constructed both look solid. I check the placement of each piece of hardware for the tenth time. The force on both pieces of hardware is evenly distributed with a length of sling. I check the knot that joins the two ropes and the carabiner to which they're clipped. The ropes aren't twisted. I shove two parallel bights of rope through my rappel device, clip the bights to a locking 'biner extended from my harness with a sling, and take a long stare at the hookup to make sure I haven't fucked it up. I look up, and J. Jay pops half a chocolate bar into my mouth. It's the most incredible gesture: Here, now, there is no energy for sympathy. I accept J. Jay's kindness without mention. We are both cold, we are both thirsty, we are both hungry, and tired, our hands battered and painful—these are the ground rules. We are both afraid, but the only way I can take care of myself and my share of the common tasks is to know that J. Jay (or Jim, or Stefan, or Charlie, or Alex) takes care of himself and covers his share, a set of facts that makes the chocolate bar gesture all the more generous.

I chomp at the chocolate while I double- and triple-check the anchor and my rappel hookup. J. Jay's eyes peer out through his goggles to do the same. I still chomp as I unclip from the anchor and lower myself away. I swallow and spit, eyes scoping down for the next stance. I can't see much detail in the storm, but I have a fairly good idea where I'm going—I memorized this terrain when we climbed it on the way up. The wind treats me like a scabrous growth, picking, pushing, poking, scratching, worrying, shoving. Soon the clouds will warm to rain, and that will be worse.

I lower myself down the vertical wall and find the next stance about 180 feet below. To free my hands I knot the ends of the rappel ropes around my thigh and whale in a piton—a "baby angle" about the size of a pocketknife—with my ice hammer. The baby pings beautifully up the register of sound as I hammer it into a half-inch-wide crack. A foot and a half away the crack is a little wider, and there I set an aluminum wedge about the size of a sink stopper. I thread a sling through both pieces, knot and twist it to distribute my weight to each piece, clip myself to the sling with my daisy chain, and dismantle my rappel so J. Jay can come down.

A pause. For a moment I have nothing to do. I crane my neck up to watch for J. Jay, and the wind rabbit-punches my kidneys. I wince and turn and take a long look out and across the wall into the maelstrom of storm. The dark gray-brown granite drops precipitously to the snow that slopes away from its base—600 feet to go. Just the barest hints of the black streaks on the glacier that fills the valley floor thousands of feet below are visible through the gray blur of angry, angry sky. The world is elemental: wind, cloud, snow, stone, and sound rioting with unfettered glee. The storm rages with utter indifference, without vendetta. It rages because that's what it was born to do. Well braced, I take a photo, but the storm cares not one whit for me. If it crushes me then it's my own damn fault. I could have had the sense to stay home.

J. Jay arrives, clips to the new anchors, derigs his rappel, and we're under siege as we pull the ropes through the carabiner hooked to the anchor far above. A ferocious updraft roars up the wall and grabs the rope as it falls through the anchor. The updraft won't let the rope fall. It holds the rope out at full length, and the end of the rope whips back and forth in the blur of storm nearly 200 feet over our heads, dancing like an angry snake.

"Fuck, pull!" We reel in the bottom of the rope as fast as we can. The gust releases its hold on the end of the rope and tosses it to the side. The rope falls far to our right and knots around some granite flakes that protrude from the wall about sixty feet diagonally above us.

The fight comes to its climax. It feels like the battle will never end, but it does, and many hours later we get to the tent.

•

We failed, grinding ourselves up in attempt after attempt. But failure is as fine a measure of an alpinist as any other. It is enough to try, and success is not a requirement of the alpine game: Survival is. A climb would have no value at all were the outcome certain when the idea was conceived. We risked; but what farmer doesn't risk when he chooses a crop and sows a field? What can be said of his character when the rains don't come? No one can say that he lacked faith or zeal or that he failed in hope. He did his part and the sky did the rest. The wisdom contained in the saying "Victory and defeat are in the hands of God. You must learn to love the struggle" is a very hard lesson to learn.

A few days later I walk down the tongue of the glacier for the last time this season, burdened with fifty pounds of hardware and garbage. The storm that flings pebbles of sleet and rain at my back allows not even a parting glimpse of the peaks at the valley's head. But it doesn't matter as one after the other my boots grind up the distance toward home; I remember the incomparable mountains and the mighty valley, even as they neglect to remember me.

There is a tree near base camp, a scruffy southern beech, stunted and quite unspectacular, that stands apart from its fellows. I visit it whenever I am in the range, and I check in with it as I begin and end each of my alpine labors in the Torre Valley. It is gnarled and twisted and has few leaves; its roots furrow rocky soil; it casts an insignificant shadow. This year its leaves have all turned, its summer already long past while other trees yet cling to many green leaves. Through the years it hasn't grown, although perhaps it is a bit thicker. I envy this little tree, for it does what I lack the courage to do: It lives its whole life subject to the fierce wind of Patagonia.

A MONDAY AFTERNOON IN SOUTHERN CALI-
fornia, and I couldn't be farther from a Patagonian storm.
Late-winter sun shines in through the window and warms my
back. I work the e-mail and the telephone, and try to push
forward my writing career. Pictures of my wife with penguins
in South Africa, of Yosemite's El Capitan, and of a few Patagonian highlights hang on the wall. The radio plays pop tunes.
I fight the temptation to pick up a book, to get up and make
a cup of tea, or to reread the spring training statistics on the
sports page.

The phone rings. I pick it up.

"Hey, mate, what gives?" It's Andrew Lindblade and his
thick Australian accent. "Me and Ath are in New York. Got a
few hours layover at LAX on our way back to Oz from France.
Can you meet us? The Frogs just gave us the Piolet d'Or. Can't
bloody believe it."

"Christ, what were they thinking? Congrats."

The Piolet d'Or—the golden ice axe—is an award the
French Alpine Club hands out for each year's most outstand-

ing mountaineering accomplishment. Thalay Sagar's North Face in India's Garwhal Himalaya had for fifteen years rejected a slew of international alpine talent. Andrew and his partner Athol Whimp bagged it last September. They were flown to France, where they convened alongside the handful of other nominated teams for the awards ceremony. As token foreigners they figured they had no chance of winning the prize from supposedly jingoistic French judges. To their utter amazement, Athol and Andrew carried off the award. Wined, dined, and feted by the French, Ath and Andy partied it up in France, and then again in New York City as they made their way home.

I said I'd be glad to meet them, copied their flight info, and hung up.

There are few mountain souls, but Aussie Andrew Lindblade and Kiwi Athol Whimp are certainly two, both of them hard, hard men, two of the best of the modern alpine breed, equally excellent on rock, ice, or snow, and steeled to meet the world's hardest mountains. Happy circumstance put Athol on top of Cerro Torre at about the same hour that Boris and I stood on Fitzroy. Circumstances just as happy found us celebrating success a few nights later in the same Chaltén bar. Dark-haired Athol Whimp sat in the corner and quietly polished off his drinks. I remember the long look in his eyes, a look that reminded me of the old photos of Marines just off the tough islands in the Pacific. I doubt that a hundred Cerro Torres add up to a single Iwo Jima, but Athol had just soloed Cerro Torre, the second man to successfully do so.

As he warmed to the company and his cups, Athol encouraged me to chase my Fitzroy climb with an attempt on Cerro Torre, but I said no way. I was done with mountains for the season. There is such a thing as too much luck, and it's just as crucial to know when to walk away as it is to know when to throw yourself into the fray. I'd already had too much luck, and Cerro Torre could wait.

In Yosemite late that year I was switching campsites in Camp 4 in order to skirt the Park Service's two-week camping limit. I lugged my pitched tent across camp and came face-to-face with Athol making a similarly motivated relocation. Athol was on the hardman's tour of Yosemite's best and biggest rock climbs with Andrew, who had also climbed Cerro Torre and Fitzroy's North Pillar. I was fighting my way back into climbing shape after six months of traveling in South America post-Fitzroy. A storm moved into Yosemite, and we spent the next days yarning and drinking hot chocolates and beer in the Mountain Room Bar. Athol doesn't waste energy in useless action. I've never seen him in explosive action, but I don't doubt the flip side of his stillness—the efficient, determined man in action, making continuous quick, serious, and correct decisions. The man is a warrior, and an unsung hero of the alpine tribe.

Deadlines hemmed me in and I was practically too broke to put gas in the truck, but I dropped it all the next day and headed to L.A. What I wanted, and knew that I had to have, was a few hours with other people on the alpine team.

I fought the traffic, pulled Ath and Andrew out of the Los Angeles airport, and took them to Venice Beach. There wasn't much action on a weekday winter afternoon, so we installed ourselves under the awning of a hamburger joint, a little oasis in the alpine desert of Southern California.

"How was Thalay?" I asked.

"Bloody grim." Smiles and beers all around.

Grim. And a movie of wind; blowing snow; cold, numb fingers and toes; shattered nerves; day after day in the grip of fear; strain; wasted bodies; and battered hands and ropes played through my mind. So many things understood between us and taken for granted in a single word. The immense personal sacrifices that go into making big trips happen. The work, the training, the tension, the buildup. There was so much that we didn't have to say.

Great as it was to see these friends again, to hear their stories of Thalay Sagar, to rattle off a few of my own, and to talk of the great mountains of the world, what made the huge impression on me was being with people who *know*. We sat at a table on the shores of the Pacific while the sun lowered off to the west, and talking mountains with these two meant there was no need, no desire, to ask or explain why. Among the three of us, there was no argument about the value of the alpine life. We had all chosen.

At six P.M. I put the two of them on a plane and I was alone again in L.A.

I N J A N U A R Y 1 9 7 4 "T H E L E C C O S P I D E R S ," A N
Italian team led by Casimiro Ferrari, realized Walter Bonatti and Carlo Mauri's vision and climbed the West Face of
Cerro Torre. Depending on whether one accepts Maestri's
1959 claim to the summit, and whether one recognizes the le-
gitimacy of his 1970 creation of the Compressor Route, Cerro
Torre had been climbed for either the third, second, or first
time. The Spiders published a brief story and a few photos in
Britain's *Mountain* magazine. John Bragg read the account, and
the West Face of the Torre captured a chunk of terrain in his
imagination.

John Bragg and Jim Donini went to Patagonia in 1975 and
attempted the first ascent of Cerro Standhardt, the right-hand
of the three Torres. They came close, but didn't make it to the
top. In 1976 Bragg and Donini and Jay Wilson made the first
ascent of Torre Egger, the middle Torre. Back from that trip,
Donini got married. His new wife was pregnant and due in
January 1977—smack in the middle of the Patagonian summer season. Bragg and Wilson had no such commitments, and

they decided to return to Patagonia to attempt the second ascent of the Torre's West Face.

The Lecco Spiders had laid siege to the Torre's West Face in classic expedition style, the style used to make most Himalayan climbs. Twelve climbers worked in relays to establish the route. Thousands of feet of fixed rope were rigged and left in situ to ease travel between well-stocked camps and to secure the team's line of retreat. Lightweight ladders were fixed over some sections. Whenever the weather permitted, a group of point men pushed the route to a new high point and added to the line of fixed ropes, and on January 13, Daniele Chiappa, Mario Conti, Casimiro Ferrari, and Giuseppe Negri stood on top. Cerro Torre had at last been climbed without controversy.

Alpine-style climbing—a small team ascending in a single push with just the one load of food and equipment that they can carry—appealed to John Bragg as the most interesting blend of the physical and mental aspects of alpinism. The year after the Torre Egger climb, Bragg and Jay Wilson returned to Patagonia to undertake the second ascent of the Torre's West Face in alpine style, eschewing the siege tactics of the Spiders. They were intimidated by the incredible remoteness of the West Face, they didn't have any detailed knowledge of the route, and they didn't know what hardships to expect from the ice cap, so Jay and John decided to make up a threesome and enlisted Dave Carman of Wyoming.

Today, Patagonia feels like the edge of the world. In the 1970s, it *was* the edge of the world. "Back then," says Bragg, "I remember being pleased that I had just managed to get to the mountains of Patagonia." From the end of the road it took Bragg, Wilson, and Carman two weeks of horrendous load carrying to get all their food and equipment out to the back side of Cerro Torre, the base of the West Face. They dug a snow cave at the bottom of the face and prepared their ascent. A few days later they started up.

John Bragg had graduated from Harvard with a physics degree, but he wasn't just a brain, he was also a hell of an athlete, and in the seventies he was at the top of his game. "I was pretty fit in those days," says Bragg. (He's pretty fit these days, too.) They started up in good weather, but it didn't develop into a long good spell. At the end of their first day they climbed the Helmet, the massive mushroom of rime ice halfway up the route that had stopped Bonatti and Mauri's attempt twenty years before, but the weather clamped down, and the trio sat through two and a half stormy days in an ice cave. When the wind abated and the clouds evaporated, they tackled the upper tower, and spent their fourth night in a natural ice grotto under a rime mushroom high up the Torre's west shoulder, six or seven hundred feet below the summit. Clouds socked in the peak the next day, but there wasn't much wind and they went for the top. They emerged from the clouds near the top of Cerro Torre. The mountain protruded from a sea of soft clouds like an icy finger. Bragg, Carman, and Wilson climbed up and around tenuous and treacherous and difficult formations of rime and made it to the top. Wind and storm caught them on the way down, but they survived and returned to civilization having made one of the great Patagonian ascents.

•

The phone rings.

It's Thomas Ulrich calling from Switzerland to propose that I join him, Stefan Siegrist, and another Swiss climber I don't know to attempt the first winter ascent of Cerro Torre's West Face. We chatter on about this and that, while a deeper part of my brain tries to decide whether or not I should go.

My plan to climb in Pakistan in June and July went in the tank a week ago when my German partner bailed out. I have spent hours working the phone in the last seven days; it has proved impossible to find a replacement for such a long and expensive expedition at this late date, but my time is already set aside. Summer in Pakistan is winter in Patagonia. The schedule works.

But Cerro Torre . . . again? The West Face? In winter? The West Face is a legendary climb, occupying a place in modern climbing circles like the North Face of Switzerland's Eiger did in the 1950s, and most everybody in the core of the alpine circle is in some way drawn to the route. Few actually decide to go. I know its history well; I've heard and read stories about it for years. The route has been climbed only seven times before, and never in the winter. My ego would love to do it.

It will be brutal work just to get to the base of the West Face. We'll have to haul our loads up a huge pass and go out onto the ice cap to access the back side of the range. The ice cap fascinates me. Most of the time it's invisible, hidden behind the rampart of the Andes like a lost world. For the last five years I have looked out to the ice cap from high up the flanks of the peaks, but I've never actually been out there. I'd love to go, but I'm intimidated by the idea of doing such a difficult and dangerous route from so isolated a start point.

Realistically, what are our chances of pulling off such an ascent with an untried multinational team? They can't be better than about 20 percent. Patagonia is a scary place. It'll be worse out on the ice cap, and if anything goes drastically wrong, if one of us gets hurt, it will be damn near impossible to drag the stricken climber to help and safety fast enough to make a difference. Thomi and Stefan are fabulous climbers—I know, I've seen them in action—and we get along, but we've never actually shared a rope. There is no hard evidence that we'll work well as a team, and I don't even know the fourth guy. Multinational expeditions are notoriously unsuccessful; language problems and differences of mountaineering approach have historically torn them apart.

The first American ascent of this, the first British ascent of that, those strike me as meaningless distinctions. Nationalism is one of the stupidest forces in mountaineering. But there is a strong American connection to the Torre's West Face, one that feels personal to me. Bragg and Wilson feature in dozens of Donini's tales, and with Dave Carman, their alpine-style ascent of the West Face is one of the great Patagonian stories. Bragg's legacy on the East Coast, where I learned to climb, is enormous. I've been chasing his name through guidebooks for years. I met Bragg at a trade show a few years ago and we spent an hour discussing things Patagonian. Unfortunately, I couldn't also interview Jay Wilson—he was killed in a mid-eighties climbing accident.

The third ascent of the West Face was done in 1984 by two Boulder climbers, Mike Bearzi and Eric Winkleman. I never met either one when I lived there, but the community of climbers is small, and we have a bunch of friends in common, friends who speak highly of both. Jon Krakauer and Dan Cauthorn did it next. At the time, I had never met either, but I read and enjoyed their published accounts. Donini knows them both from his years of living in Seattle and swears that they're great guys.

I know it's tenuous, but I do feel a tie to these guys who bet their asses on the West Face. These guys are part of my alpine village. The first winter ascent of Cerro Torre's West Face? That's a good project. It would be nice to keep some part of it in the family.

I don't know exactly what to expect from the Patagonian winter, but I have a visceral understanding of how much pain an expedition to the Torre's West Face will involve. I've heard stories that the winter weather in Patagonia is more stable than it is at other times, but I'm dubious. I don't personally know anybody who has climbed there in winter, and any weather advantage will probably be offset by deep winter cold and long nights.

So why should I go and try to climb Cerro Torre's West Face when I've already climbed the mountain once? Because it's huge and I'll probably fail. Because it's huge and I might succeed, and I'd like to find out if I can get down from so high up and so far gone. Because of the guys in my climbing community who have been there before me and because I like the idea of doing the first winter ascent. My previous dose of the Torre, that summer campaign on the Compressor Route, rocked my world, but it nearly broke me, too, and Cerro Torre stands tall in my mind every single day. If I return to that most perfect of mountains perhaps I can plumb other depths of that same emotional well. And also because maybe, just maybe, I can knock out those last few yards to the top of the final summit mushroom that I missed the last time I was up there.

"All right, Thomi, I'm in."

.

My skis slice a trail in the surface crust of snow. The world is vast, and cold, and, except for the sound of heavy breathing and skis scraping over snow, the world is utterly silent. I take deep, measured breaths like an endurance athlete—in slow and out fast—and my many layers of clothing are damp from sweat. I'm tired, but I could keep this pace all night. Seven months have gone by since I agreed to join Thomas Ulrich and attempt to make the first winter ascent of Cerro Torre's West Face, and now he and I ski side by side up the Southern Patagonian Ice Cap under the light of winter's first full moon. We are like a pair of oxen pulling a wagon, dragging a sled loaded with food and equipment. Thomi and I have a twenty-foot piece of rope rigged into a big V to haul the sled. The base of the V is hitched to the front of the sled, and the two free ends are clipped to the back of our climbing harnesses. The grade is gentle uphill, unfortunately just steep enough that our skis and the sled won't glide. The scrape and squeak of the skis and the in-out labor of our lungs is just a bubble of noise in this soundless Patagonian sea.

I've never been in a landscape so big. We're skiing north over the upper reaches of Glaciar Viedma (which drains into the western end of Lago Viedma many miles behind us) toward El Círculo de los Altares, the Cirque of the Altars, from which rises Cerro Torre's West Face— the one aspect of the mountain that I've never seen. The sky is clear black, and the moonlight gives it a bright sheen that only the brightest stars can penetrate. The snow surface of the ice cap is silver gray and we can see for miles. To the west, gray and black mountain shapes bound the other side of the Viedma Glacier, while to our right and much closer at hand is the long line of the Cerro Adela peaks. Up ahead on the right is the mouth of the cirque, a short U-shaped valley that feeds from the west faces of the three Torres out into the ice cap.

Thomi and I ski for another hour, until we can make out the others pitching camp where the side valley meets the main stream of the Viedma Glacier. The top of Cerro Torre pokes over the snowy mountains in the foreground, the highest spire in this alpine cathedral. By midnight Thomi and I are with the others in camp, and the three Torres—Cerro Standhardt, Torre Egger, and Cerro Torre—are stark cutout shapes that stand blue-black across the top of the cirque. A silver aura of moonlight wraps the summits. They are so big and we are so very, very small. Here, out on the ice cap in winter, we are lost on an icy sea at the very edge of the world.

When I first met Thomi during the Cerro Torre campaign, he had a shaggy head of thick hair. Now, four years later, most of it is gone, even though he's a year younger than me. Of all the people I know, Thomas Ulrich might be the best at making things happen. This entire undertaking is his brainchild, and in fine Swiss tradition he is an incredible organizer. Married and the father of two, Thomi has a child's sense of humor coupled to his relentless drive. Thomi is a world-class adventure photographer, and he wanted to make this climb in winter because it hadn't been done and because we would be alone in the Patagonian Andes.

David Fasel, who is twenty-seven, is the member of our group whom I had never met before, and Thomi picked our fourth wisely. David works hard, but he doesn't take life too seriously. He realized in April that he didn't want to spend his adult life in the cubicle world of the software industry, so he quit his job to come on this expedition. In the future he plans to work as a guide and devote his life to the mountains. David is lean, fit, and not too tall, but his pack is always heavy and he does his work without complaint.

Stefan Siegrist is a hotshot climber, and a seriously good-looking bastard to boot. He's got those blond, boyish features that give women fits. Of the four of us, Stefan is the best climber on extreme rock and ice, and he makes his living as a mountain guide. Under normal circumstances he's strong enough to drag all of us to the summit, but on this expedition he has a serious motivational problem. Right before we left, his girlfriend told Stef that she had been diagnosed with cancer. Stef was stunned, grief-stricken, and he hasn't yet recovered from the shock, but his girlfriend insisted that he join the expedition. "Do it for me," she said. After much soul-searching and a huge push from her, Stefan decided to come south, but now that he's here he is tortured by the feeling that he should be back in Switzerland, and he has to struggle to push himself on. A week ago he was physically ill, racked by fever and chills, and I'm sure that his internal torture brought on the sickness.

I'm the old man of the group at age thirty-three and I've been living for the last two years in decidedly non-alpine terrain on the coast of Southern California.

The last nine days passed in a blur of physical effort, a daily grind reminiscent of Ranger School. We are lugging a mountain of food and equipment toward the base of Cerro Torre. Twenty-five days of food for four people is the heaviest chunk, but with the winter camping and climbing gear I bet this stuff weighs more than five hundred pounds. We slogged monster loads through forests, across a frozen lake, four times up a 3,000-foot pass, across rock moraines, and then, finally, this morning out onto the huge Viedma Glacier. Even with help from three Argentine friends—Alejandro Caparrós, Max O'Dell, and Gerardo Javier Spisso—and the use of local gaucho Don Guerra's packhorses for two days, this labor is backbreaking. The heavy hauling, the constant cold, the wind, and the long hours of deep-winter darkness are our major complaints. Our minor ones include blisters, ankles swollen by uncomfortable plastic mountaineering boots, freeze-dried food, no showers, smelly clothes, and instant coffee. I can't believe I let myself get talked out of bringing real coffee. Leaving the long warm days of a California summer to land smack in the middle of the shocking cold and darkness of a Patagonian winter was a systemic jolt with which I'm just beginning to come to grips.

With camp pitched in the snow I crawl into the tent I'm sharing with Thomi, snuggle into my thick down sleeping bag, and rub my thighs together to generate some warmth. I fluff some spare clothes to make a pillow, roll onto my side, and try to clear my mind of the black thoughts gnawing at me. Things are not going well. The work is brutally hard, and Stefan's struggle for motivation rubs off on us all. We have a language problem that often makes me feel like an outsider. Our expedition is barely holding itself together, and we haven't even gotten on the mountain yet.

To me, laughter is as important as food to the success of an expedition, but among us it can take ten minutes to bring off a simple piece of adolescent humor. David, Thomi, and Stefan speak Swiss German and conversational English. I have only a few stock phrases of Swiss German. I feel split off from the group when the other three babble back and forth in Swiss German and then translate the bare bones for me. All of them are making a huge effort, I know, but I feel a sense of aloneness that I've never felt on an expedition before. Usually I'm gregarious and outgoing on expeditions; this time out I'm much more introverted. I'm just beginning to discover how much I depend on humor to manage my fear and stress.

A wind starts blowing in the wee hours, and the next dawn—which comes at about nine A.M.—is frigid and blustery under a sunless gray sky. We decide to wait here for better weather while Alejandro, Max, and Gerardo pack up and ski off toward Paso Marconi to the north and their return to civilization in Chaltén. Thomi, Stefan, David, and I play cards in the tent all day.

The wind stops and the clouds thin before sunset, and light, soft as a baby's blanket, filters through the parting mists to color the Torre tender pink. The West Face above us looks gentle and inviting, an alpine paradise, and the exact opposite of the foreboding sunset impression I get when I'm on the other side of the mountain. Tomorrow we climb.

We get up early, but take hours to break camp, and by the time we get moving the sun is ready to rise. It's a grim dawn, cold, and without a trace of Cerro Torre's sunset mood. The west faces of the three Torres are iron gray, and the sun burns a line of infernal fire atop Cerro Torre, a full vertical mile above us. We trudge toward it and I think about the route—I know the details because I've pored over all the published accounts of ascents made in the warmer seasons. I can see many of the prominent features from here, close to the base of the Filo Rosso (the Pink Ridge).

From here it's a long way, but mostly easy, to the Col of Hope, the high col that divides Cerro Torre from Cerro Adela. The ice slope to the col is funnel-shaped, with the narrow end at the top, terrain perfectly designed to focus the power of a storm through the col. Then the route turns left and climbs more moderate ice to a flat platform below a 200-foot-tall blob of vertical rime nicknamed "the Helmet"—the first desperate climbing on the West Face. The Helmet is notoriously difficult, and it worries us.

The west side of the Torre faces squarely into the winds that blast in from the Pacific, and it is festooned with monstrous formations of rime ice. These rime mushrooms grow into wild, twisted shapes; the biggest are the size of houses. They are almost impossible—and always terrifying—to climb. Often the rime can't support body weight. Our route avoids the rime as much as possible and weaves up between the mushrooms, linking solid stretches of blue, gray, or translucent ice.

Easy ground connects the top of the Helmet with the base of the upper tower of the Torre, but from there it's all hard. The route up the upper tower climbs a massive dihedral from the Helmet at the bottom right to the west shoulder of Cerro Torre at the upper left. The last 200 feet of the dihedral is a plumb vertical headwall. From the shoulder about 500 feet of steep ice reaches a little notch 200 feet below the top, and that last 200-foot-tall mushroom of gruesome rime has the most fearsome reputation of any pitch on the route. If any of the crux sections—the Helmet, the headwall, or the mushroom pitch to the top—prove much more difficult in winter than they are in the summer, we may not be able to climb them.

We start up from the base of the Filo Rosso, and right from the beginning our teamwork is awful; each of us seems to have an individual agenda, and those four agendas draw and quarter the team. My goddamn ice boots are way too big—because I was too timid to complain to the company that gave me them—and when I front-point, my heels practically lift out of the boots. The steeper the terrain, the worse it feels. The insecure feeling destroys my confidence and won't let me climb relaxed. The winter isolation gnaws at me, and I think my partners are taking unnecessary risks on moderate terrain. I bitch them

out for not putting in ice screws to protect easy terrain, slopes I'd normally solo with confidence. I am afraid, plain and simple, and I can't
find any humor in which to drown the fear. On what I interpret as
David's explicit, face-to-face instructions, I unfix a rope and clip it to
my harness in order to drag the rope to the next higher anchor. Moments later I yell, "Stop! Stop!" as David begins to commit his weight
to the newly unfixed (and unsafe) rope. Disaster is averted, but I dread
any situation where we have to reach a complicated and serious decision yelling through a storm from opposite ends of a 200-foot rope. To
make matters worse, we are climbing at the pace of slugs. I feel no
alpine freedom; rather I feel trapped, way out here on the fine edge of
beyond. All of us are stressed—this place, despite its beauty, is
lethal—and somehow the worst side of each of us comes out. Thomi's
attitude seems autocratic, arrogant, and inconsiderate, and he and Stefan, the best of friends back home, are at each other's throats. David is
quiet and withdrawn, Stef doesn't want to be here, and I am a fucking
coward.

We take all day to climb the bottom third of the route—miserable
progress over easy terrain—and spend the night in a snow hole 1,000
feet below the Col of Hope. The next day we climb to the Helmet.

I kneel on the platform below the Helmet in the late afternoon
and shovel out our bivy site while David tackles the steep rime ice of
the Helmet. Stefan has already failed twice to get up steep rime
grooves farther left. David has decided to try the right skyline, which
might be just a little off vertical. I long to be anywhere but here. I sit
back on my heels and look out over the ice cap. The view is mind-
boggling, but today the Andes make no impression. These have been
the two blackest days of my alpine career, and I've barely got my
emotions under control. I'd give years off my life to teleport back to
California.

Where the rime is steepest David pounds several of our three-foot-long aluminum stakes into the crumbly rime and uses them as points of aid. The climbing is tenuous and hard, and the stakes pounded into the rime offer only scant protection. If he falls, he's likely to rip out the stakes. David's progress is slow, but he gets it done, and when he's finally on top of the Helmet he anchors the end of the rope, unties, and rappels down to join the rest of us on the platform at the Helmet's base.

Sunset is calm and clear, and the low-angle light of sunset and winter paints the whole world in soft tones of red and orange. If tomorrow is a fine day we will press on with our climb, but I don't want to continue. I feel a creeping doom. Alone in my sleeping bag I try to fall asleep, and I catch myself almost praying for storm.

At three o'clock in the morning, an hour before we are to wake up, I feel the first breath of wind. By the time the alarm beeps the wind is blowing steadily and no stars are visible over the mountains to the west. The group decision is to wait till dawn and assess the weather then, but I know Patagonia, and I'm sure the weather is crapping out. We'll be going down. I tuck myself back into my sleeping bag, roll over, and sleep like a baby until eight.

Sure enough, the dawn sky shows signs of an incoming storm. We could press on—we might even make it to the top—but if a strong storm does materialize we'll be caught at the wrong end of the Torre. We'd probably go for it from here in summer but decide not to chance it in winter. We opt for retreat, and things immediately begin to improve. Thomi suggests a beautifully efficient system for descending with four people, and I go to the point of the action, down first to build each anchor, finally able to demonstrate some alpine competence.

Descent takes most of the day. At the bottom of the West Face, in the glacier's moat at the base of the Filo Rosso, we dump our food and climbing gear into three big waterproof bags, wedge them under a boulder, load essentials into our packs, tie the packs into the two sleds, and start skiing. We're aiming for a small hut left years ago by glacier researchers on a lateral moraine beside the Viedma Glacier. The hut is at least twelve miles away. Darkness falls. The wind is building and it's blowing a steady fifteen knots down-glacier by the time we turn the corner out of El Círculo de los Altares. The turn puts the wind at our backs and the glacier slopes ever so slightly downhill in the direction we want to go. The clouds that cover the sky shut off the moonlight. We stop to put on our headlamps and to take the skins off the bottom of our mountaineering skis. The skins have a nap like the hair on a short-haired dog. The little hairs point backward and stop us from sliding to the rear when we go uphill, but the skins do add a lot of friction. With the skins off, our skis glide beautifully over the hard frozen snow. I unzip my jacket, spread it wide like a sail, and arch my back. The wind catches my jacket and shoves me gliding along. I hardly move a muscle as I coast about ten miles down-glacier, pushed by the wind, chasing my Swiss partners and the pool of light cast by my headlamp.

We arrive at the crude hut around midnight. The hut sits at the end of a little valley the size of a few football fields bounded on two adjacent sides by the rock walls of a moraine. A little stream flows in front and drains into a frozen pond a hundred feet from the front door. On the other side of the pond, the earth rises to meet the western slopes of Cerro Huemul. The hut is perhaps twelve feet wide and maybe twenty feet long and it is floored in concrete. The walls are made of tin lined on the inside with posterboard. A high-water mark four feet up the posterboard shows that the hut is subject to frequent floods, but I don't think we've got anything to worry about in midwinter. There is no heat. The hut is a miserable little place. Living inside it is like living in an icebox, and the only way to stay warm is to wear all of our clothes and eat constantly, but it does put a roof over our heads and there is much more room to move around in here than there would be inside a tent.

By daylight, the storm is fully developed, snow driven by incredible wind with temperatures far below freezing. I go outside and decide that this full-blown roaring forties winter rager is every bit as ferocious as its summer counterpart. We made a good decision not to press on from the Helmet—we might have finished the climb, but if we did, this storm would have caught us when we were most vulnerable and at the maximum distance from flat ground. So far, I haven't detected a weather benefit to the Patagonian winter. The storm winds are every bit as strong as those I have experienced in the spring and summer months, and the winter days are shorter and much, much colder. If there's a single winter advantage, it's that I feel that I can see the winter storms developing about twenty-four hours in advance. In summer, the sky can change from deep blue and windless into a raging gray blur in just a few hours. There is an edge in winter's fair warning.

The warmth of our cooking and our combined body heat wake up the pack of lauchas—those pesky Patagonian mice—who hibernate in the walls of the hut. After dark the lauchas find a smorgasbord of table scraps at their disposal, and they root through the foil wrappers of our freeze-dried food and scavenge through our dirty plastic dishes. Their little noises torment us all night.

We take stock of our situation and decide to try to make another attempt. The long nights and the cold have chewed up our supply of headlamp batteries. Because the winter days are so brief, we absolutely must be able to make progress in the dark. Thomi and Stefan ski back to Chaltén to round up more headlamp batteries. David and I don't fancy the arduous round-trip. Despite the recent problems, I don't want to return to civilization, I don't want to break the spectacular isolation, and for me it'd be too easy to quit if I went back. The two of us decide to stay put and wait out the storm in the hut.

The storm outside blasts by in a duochromatic blur of gray and white. The eight or nine hours of light are frigid inactive torture. The fifteen or sixteen hours of darkness are much, much worse. I finish my only book halfway through the second day. I write my way through my only notebook in the days that follow, then fill the back sides of each page, then start working my way from front to back in the margins. David rolls and smokes cigarettes and we brew drinks, stretch the time between meals as long as we can endure, and step outside the hut to piss or fetch water from the stream.

Time in the cold hut is endless, and David and I build a supply of stock jokes, ones we revisit whenever one of us needs a laugh. We get to know each other, and once we do I recognize David for a kindred spirit, as intent as I am on plowing a unique furrow through life.

For two nights we are kept awake by the scrapings of the mice as they ferret their way through our garbage. Trying to sleep fourteen hours a night is hard enough, but it's made impossible as hour after hour the little monsters drag our empty foil meal pouches across the concrete floor. I am bed sore from the long hours on my back. We don't have enough candles or headlamp batteries to break more than an hour or two of darkness each night. I've been reluctant to build the bucket-and-spinning-pole mousetrap because the only container the right size is our largest cook pot, but a laucha runs through my hair in the middle of the third night, and I decide that I don't care about the pot and get up to build the trap. I dismantle a ski pole to use as the rotating axle, fill the pot halfway with water, and carefully prepare the doomsday device. David is fascinated by the trap. He lurks in his sleeping bag a few feet from the pot, holding his headlamp at the ready so he can inspect the results.

Plop! Plop! Plop! It's a mouse massacre—the trap is as efficient as a guillotine, and we quickly score three victims. David flashes his headlamp on the drowning beast after each plop, beside himself with glee. "Teach you to keep us awake!"

David's antics have me thrashing around in my sleeping bag, crumpled up with laughter. This is by far the best entertainment we've had out here.

When we're finally quiet and the lights are off we hear another mouse scurrying around in our trash. "Die, you terrorist," mutters my partner from the dark depths of his sleeping bag.

Soon there is another splash and David is quick with the light. The light hits the trap just in time to showcase a three-inch mouse as he springs from the water to the rim, pulls himself over the edge, and escapes.

Ten minutes later David spotlights the trap again and sees the same mouse escape.

"He got away *again*," yells David. "He is a Supermouse!"

In the morning we examine the trap. Three drowned mouse corpses are frozen into a block of solid ice. I heat the pot over the stove to dislodge the big ice cube and set the block and its embedded victims outside the hut. We decide that the Supermouse was probably vaulting from the corpses of his drowned fellows, and figure that we'll get him with an empty trap in the coming night.

The storm continues, and the next night the mouse again and again escapes the trap and torments us with his foraging. The following night is a repeat performance. The Supermouse falls in our trap over and over but keeps making good his escapes. Then, in the wee hours, when David and I are finally sound asleep, the Supermouse launches his counterattack.

Just as it starts to get light, David wakes up and stirs to roll his first smoke of the day.

"Supermouse, soon you will be a dead mouse!" sings David at the top of his lungs in the style of the heavy-metal bands he so admires. I'm shocked awake.

"What the . . . ?"

"Aaahhhh," he yells, "that little fucker ate half my tobacco!"

"Supermouse, soon you will be a dead mouse!" David roars his tuneless battle song over and over, obsessed with revenge. From any detached perspective it must sound moronic, but out here on the edge of the ice cap I collapse with laughter every time.

David fixes me with berserk eyes. "Greg, you must build me a *supertrap* for the *Supermouse.*"

I'm happy to comply, but there isn't much to work with out here. In the back corner of the hut is a dirty expedition barrel filled with odds and ends left here by previous occupants of the hut. I dig through the detritus and can't seem to come up with the raw materials to match my vision for a supertrap. I'm sitting back nursing a cup of chicken soup when the concept hits me—the barrel itself will serve.

So that night before we go to sleep I build a megatrap with the barrel in place of the bucket of water. The barrel is about the size of a fifty-five-gallon drum, and since it reaches up to my waist I don't see any need to fill it with water. I use a ski as the ramp to the rim and a full ski pole as the spinning axis. David eyes the device with approval and wails his Supermouse dirge.

I wake at midnight, startled by a *sh-sh-sh-donk, sh-sh-sh-donk* sound. I lie in my sleeping bag confused and hear the sound again. I sit up—*sh-sh-sh-donk*—then twist on my headlamp and train it on the trap.

"David, David, get up! We got him!"

The Supermouse is trapped in the barrel, but he jumps and scrambles with his little claws *sh-sh-sh* about an inch short of the rim before he falls back to the bottom with a *donk.*

The mouse vaults again, and again comes up a little bit short. "Do something, it's getting away!"

David roars and catapults from his sleeping bag. He comes up with a container and dumps the fluid into the barrel. I think he plans to drown the beast and yell that there's more water on the table, then watch gobsmacked as David flicks a lit match into the barrel behind the fluid and the barrel *whoosh*es into flame. Flames jet eight feet out of the barrel, right up to the roof.

"You crazy Swiss fuck! You poured our stove fuel on him."

"Burn, burn, burn, you bastard, burn," howls David.

The whole hut looks to go up in flames. I scramble out of my sleeping bag.

"A supertrap for the Supermouse!" David dances a war dance around the barrel. The hut fills with oily black smoke.

I pull on my boot liners and join David in the dance. We roar and howl and laugh and chant until our voices break and the fire burns down in the barrel. The fire dies out and it's dark again and we laugh and laugh until I'm on all fours laughing and choking on the smoke.

We fish the charred corpse of the Supermouse out of the barrel— the fried remains are about the size of a roll of film—prop the hut's door open, and peg the dead beast to one of the hut's guy wires with a clothespin. Outside it's blustery and cold and moonlit clouds scud across the night sky. We're just wearing long underwear and the liners of our ice boots, but we jump around in the crusty snow and laugh and howl at the moonlight. Then we just stand quiet and enjoy the night until we get too cold.

The next day we derive much mirth rehashing the climactic events of the Supermouse battle, but that night—without the mouse torture—it does not prove any easier to muster fourteen hours of sleep. The night is endless.

"Shit," says David when we get up to fix breakfast, "last night was boring. We should not have killed the Supermouse."

We ache from inactivity, but by afternoon the storm seems to have lost its power. We scramble up the moraine beside the hut at dusk and examine the clear skies to the west. I think tomorrow will be a fine day; we may yet get a chance to do this thing.

After nine days stuck here on the edge of the ice cap, David and I are old friends. We haven't seen the others in a week, but we expect them with the weather change.

"David," I warn, "if those two come back from town without steaks and whiskey I will cut their throats with my plastic spoon, drink their blood, and hang their bodies next to the Supermouse."

"Don't worry," says David. "They will take care of us."

Stefan and Thomi arrive at the hut after dark. They've skied the full distance up from Chaltén in a single day, and they've got a big resupply of headlamp batteries. We will head up to the Cirque of the Altars tomorrow and hope for another climbing opportunity. They've also got thick steaks and a decanted bottle of whiskey. The expedition is saved. Stefan and Thomi take gentle sips while David and I drink the stuff like it's water. It's great to see Thomi and Stefan again. Stefan spoke to his girlfriend in Switzerland and she again urged him on, so his morale is better. We all comment on her courage. David and I recount the Battle of the Supermouse, delighting in every exquisite detail. Thomi catches Stefan's eye and they each raise an eyebrow, convinced that we've been out here too long and have gone a little crazy. Perhaps we have, but it finally feels like the four of us have jelled into a team and are eager to get to the business of climbing the West Face. And David has seen me at my alpine finest, for I am the Muhammad Ali of killing time: I am the greatest, and I admit no equal. We now understand each other; the language differences are still present, but we've found and congregated on our common ground—the love of high and wild places.

•

Forty-eight hours later we're in just such a place, 900 feet below the summit of Cerro Torre. We left the hut two days ago in clear, bitterly cold weather and skied up the ice cap to our gear stash at the base of the Filo Rosso. One of our bags was missing. We found it—and the 100 pounds of food and equipment in it—about 200 meters *uphill*. It takes two of us to lift the awkward bag. The only possible explanation is that the bag was pushed by the winds of the recent storm. We slept for six hours, got up at three A.M., and climbed the bottom two-thirds of the West Face. I solved my heel-lift problem caused by my oversized ice boots by wearing every one of my five pairs of socks. We covered the same amount of terrain in one day that took us two days on our previous attempt. We moved like a team, and we climbed with light hearts. I was, and am, scared—only a fool wouldn't be—but this time up my fear is practical, and not debilitating.

In the morning we launched ourselves at the upper tower. Now, late in the afternoon, we're up against the two-hundred-foot headwall of vertical ice that separates us from the upper west shoulder of Cerro Torre. Flat ground lies a mile of gravity-defying terrain below. A vast and savage winter Patagonian landscape of ice, snow, mountain, and sky sits just over my left shoulder, but I don't dare look. The weather is obviously deteriorating, and my psyche can't handle another eyeful of the lenticular clouds over the peaks to the west and the graying horizon beyond. To calm myself I inspect the slings, carabiners, and ice screws that anchor me to this vertiginous ice, scan the rope for tangles, and examine the belay device through which my gloved hands feed the rope to Thomi above. The battered locking carabiner clipped to the rope and belay plate is a talisman, an old and dependable companion, veteran of much shared experience. I nod to the scratched and chipped locker and touch it with my free hand. I'm obsessed with doing everything right. Still, waves of fear surge through me. Dangling here in midwinter from the headwall of Cerro Torre, crown jewel of the Patagonian Andes, I feel like an egg balanced atop a flagpole.

Thomi clings by the metal points of his two ice axes and his crampons to the sheet of vertical ice above. Two hundred feet below, David and Stefan prepare to ascend the rope to my small platform chopped out of the ice. Thomi bangs one axe into the bulletproof surface, and a dinner plate of ice shatters loose and whacks the top of my helmet. He hacks again, securely embeds his axe into the ice, and tests the placement with a tug. He kicks the front points of his crampons into the ice, and steps up while a fresh flurry of ice fragments ricochets off my head. I hunch my shoulders and shrink my neck in an effort to hide my whole body beneath my helmet.

Thunk; chunk-chunk. The noises tell me what's going on; I can't risk an upward glance for fear that falling ice will smash me in the face. We're on the cusp of realizing our dream, but this short, eight-hour July day is almost over, and we have no chance of reaching the top today.

I shiver, thinking about another long night on an icy perch with the temperature well below zero Fahrenheit. There is much to fear. We left no umbilical cord of rope strung out behind us to secure our descent. Our safety depends on a quick and efficient climb up and down. The winter cold and the few hours of daylight complicate every aspect of the climb. We need more clothing, heavier sleeping bags, more headlamp batteries, more fuel, and more calories than we would in the summer. It's a double bind, because every additional ounce means we climb slower, which in turn makes us need more gear. No one has ever been here in winter before. Will the ice above be rotten, unable to support our body weight? Is my courage equal to this task? Above all else,

I fear the return of storm. I'm afraid that we might be trying to shoe-horn this alpine blitzkrieg into one of the dreaded "almost good enough" windows of fair weather and that the next inevitable storm will catch us close to the top, and I am not confident that we can escape the fury of a full-blown winter storm. The storm that pinned us in Supermouse Hut was one of the most furious Patagonian storms that I have ever seen, and here on the Torre's West Face we look right into the teeth of the wind.

Back on Cerro Torre's headwall, the rain of ice on my helmet continues, then stops. I chance a look around. The line of clouds to the west seems a little darker, the wind a little stronger. If anything, the weather's a little more ominous than it was ten minutes ago. Thomi, suspended sixty feet above by a cord from his harness to his right ice axe, uses both hands to twist in an ice screw, an eight-inch-long, one-and-a-quarter-inch-diameter threaded hollow tube that will arrest any fall. Thomi could easily crank in a screw with one hand under normal conditions, but into this supercold, superhard winter ice it takes all his strength. The vertical ice soars 100 feet over Thomi's head.

I'm just below the upper left-hand corner of the massive dihedral, where ice-covered walls of granite come together like the pages of an open book. Far above, the biggest, most twisted rime formations on the entire peak shine a ghoulish white in the sunlight. They guard access to the summit, and they look utterly impregnable.

"Greg," Thomi coos from above with his Swiss lilt, "this is the best. This is sooo radical." I'm glad he's having such a good time; I'm so afraid I might vomit. I look down. Below and to the right, Stefan ascends the rope toward my anchor. Beneath Stefan, David waits his turn sheltered below a gargoyle of rime. I can just make him out as he ducks his head inside his yellow jacket and—improbably—calmly lights a cigarette.

Forty minutes later, Thomi picks and kicks over the top of the headwall and disappears onto the West Face's shoulder. I muster enough courage to fumble with my ascenders and follow him up the headwall. I'm panting when I reach Thomi, and beneath my two union suits, fleece sweater, insulated jacket, and storm shell, I'm bathed in greasy sweat. The sun weakly shines on me for the first time today, fifteen minutes before it drops behind the mountains to the west. The low-angle light makes the rime mushrooms shine a brilliant yellow. We're in another world.

Thomi is carrying the ascent. I've never seen a guy have such a good day in the mountains, and inspired by his performance, I claim the next lead. I head twenty feet left, then up into a groove. I'm knackered from our two full days on this hill. Steeper and steeper ice forces me to use only the front points of the crampons under the toes of my boots. I focus on making smooth, controlled swings with my axes and refuse to give in to my quivering calves.

It's six P.M. and the sun has vanished. It'll be ten A.M. before its rays touch us again. Meanwhile, I'm still leading, and any fall would result in serious injury. In gathering darkness I pick and kick my way to the end of the pitch, rig the rope to two ice screws, and descend to join my teammates. I find them digging out a bivy spot under a rime mushroom that rears up like a bandshell on a flat shelf just above the headwall. I scrape up a mound of rime along the edge to make me feel safe. I don't want to roll off in my sleep and take the death dive. As I work, my hands ache, the wind chills my sweat-damp clothing, and I think about tomorrow. More pain. I smile, remembering the scene in *Rocky III* when a journalist asks Clubber Lang, the challenger, what is his prediction for the coming fight. His answer: "Pain!" I explain it to the team. We laugh.

We arrange our sleeping perches just above the headwall. Thomi faces the blackness to the west, then turns. "Boys," he says, "I am not religious, but tonight we are in the hands of God, and when I get home, I am going to make a third kid."

He's right. If the storm holds off, we go up and finish this thing. If not, down we go.

The cooking hassles go on and on. The stove won't work well and it takes hours to melt enough rime to fill all of our water bottles. I sit in my sleeping bag and get ready for the night as I fiddle with the stove. My bag is inside a bivy sack and perched on a thin insulating pad. I put my empty backpack under my chest and shoulders to provide an extra layer between me and the rime ice below. I wear a thin and a thick union suit of long underwear, a pair of fleece pants, and my storm pants wrapped around my feet. I keep my two thickest socks on my feet and zip my three thinnest pairs where they might dry against my skin in the chest of my union suits. The cloud of body-funk that erupts from my long underwear is horrendous—I haven't showered in nearly a month. Over the union suits I wear a fleece sweater and a warm jacket. Two balaclavas wrap my head and I make a pillow out of my storm shell. The intense cold means that we must sleep with every piece of equipment that we can't let freeze, so I stuff boot liners, water bottles, headlamp, spare batteries, and the stove into my sleeping bag. When I'm finally ready I wriggle down into the bag and zip the outer bivy sack shut and draw the mummy cord of my sleeping bag tight around my double-hatted head. I'm inside the best down sleeping bag I could find, wearing top-notch expedition clothing, and I'm still not warm, but I'm not freezing either. With all the stuff crammed in with me it's like sleeping on a cobblestone bed, but I'm exhausted and I manage to fall asleep.

Hours later I awake with a cramp locking up one hamstring. I writhe around, knowing the cramp has been brought on by dehydration. I'm angry and in pain; I can't afford this kind of physical bullshit up here. When I'm able, I sit up and gently stretch my leg while I drain one of my water bottles. When I'm again under control I examine the weather: a wet, gentle breeze is still blowing and only a few stars are visible above—it's still too close to call.

At six o'clock in the morning, pulses from a wristwatch alarm shatter my sleep. I stir and fight the Velcro tabs, draw cords, and zippers that close my sleeping bag and bivy sack from the freezing air. Ice crystals, frozen onto the inside of the sack, rain onto my face and melt. A dream of lying on a beach under a hot sun with my beautiful wife, DeAnne, hangs in my mind. Outside the sleeping bag, reality is a world of ice. Automatically I check the dark sky for approaching storm. The brightest stars shine fuzzy through a layer of high clouds. A breeze tickles my nostrils with moisture and hints of pain to come. I think a storm is coming, but I think it's going to hold off just long enough. "Wake up, boys. Today we climb."

I fish my headlamp from the depths of the sleeping bag, turn it on, and fumble to fire up the stove. The midwinter sun is hours away, but with the stove hissing and roaring, I won't drop back to sleep. After an hour of tending the stove and melting rime, the Swiss are now also in a preparation frenzy. We pull on clothes, devour muesli, adjust ice boots, harnesses, and crampons, load rime and snow into the pot to fill water bottles, stuff sleeping bags and backpacks—all on the brink of what seems to be the drop off the edge of the world. We're hopeful for the top, so we leave our sleeping and cooking gear behind and pack just clothing, hardware, water, snack food, and cameras. It takes two full hours to get ready.

I serve up my best sportscaster imitation, "Clubber, what's your prediction for the fight?"

And in unison my three Swiss friends howl, "Pain!"

In two hours we climb 500 feet above our bivouac and—boom— we're face-to-face with the summit mushrooms we saw from below. They lean out and overhang the north and west faces like the prows of half a dozen *Titanic*s. If we can't find a groove up through these barriers or a traverse around them, our ascent stops right here.

Stefan takes the lead and finds a possible route down and then up around to the left. He attacks a groove while David belays and Thomi takes photos. I scan the range. The view over the rock towers and glaciers of Patagonia is sublime; the weather isn't. The lines of lenticular clouds along the mountain range to the west are thicker and blacker, and beyond is a murky torrent of approaching cloud. On all the mountains around us strong wind blows snow through cols and tears it from ridges, but for some odd reason that defies logic, here, 200 feet below the summit of Cerro Torre, I could light a match.

David looks over and asks, "What do you think?"

"I think we're gonna make it, but Patagonia is gonna make us pay."

Stefan fights his way up seventy feet of shoddy, rotten rime in the groove he's found, then finds a patch of ice solid enough to hold a screw. He clips the rope through and has David lower him back down to the belay. He's exhausted.

Thomi takes the lead and disappears up the rime groove. David feeds the rope out. Twenty minutes later a steady shower of ice chunks comes flying down from above. Thomi is hacking open the top end of a twenty-foot-long hollow tube that goes up through the heart of the steepest rime mushroom. We each follow Thomi in succession. The vertical culvert is the wildest ice feature I've ever encountered. I'm quiet with awe as I climb through it.

The culvert is the key to the climb. Thirty feet above it I join my friends on the summit of Cerro Torre. Thomi pulls his camera aside from in front of his face and uncovers a Cheshire cat grin. We hug and cavort and pummel one another's backs and take zillions of photos. I look around, and the summit geography looks pretty much the same as it did four years ago. I recognize the slot where Charlie and I spent the night, bumps in the plateau from which I took photos before, the crunchy feel of the rime beneath my boots. It is surreal to be here for a second time. Or, better said, almost on the summit for the second time. We cavort on the same plateau next to the same thirty- or forty-foot-high mushroom that stymied Charlie and me. The last mushroom leans over like a frozen breaking wave, and we can't find enough solid ice to climb to the very top. Ouch.

I can't relax. I won't relax and celebrate until we're safe below, but I soak up the view. What on earth have I done to deserve this view for a second time? The ice field and a sea of mountains stretch away north, south, and west. The sun glints off Laguna del Desierto to the left of the enormous wedge of Fitzroy. The rocky teeth of the range stand close at hand. We've been here about an hour. I bring the details into sharp focus and see that everywhere other than here is being scrubbed by fierce wind.

"Okay, boys, that's enough fun. We're out of here."

Stefan suddenly has command of his full powers. For the first time in a month, here on the summit, his physical actions are in line with his emotional desire, for every step, every exertion takes him closer to his girlfriend in Switzerland. He buries a three-foot-long aluminum stake sideways in the summit snows, ties a sling to its middle, and anchors two ropes knotted together to the sling with a snap link. We plan to stick with our previous descent system, so I get set to go down first. I clip the ropes through my rappel device, shuffle around below the anchor, and try not to think about the three-foot stake buried sideways in foamy snow that will soon support my entire 170-pound frame.

I gently ease my weight into my harness and slowly settle my full weight onto the anchor. I let myself slide down the rope a few feet and then stop. I look up at those last few yards to the absolute summit of Cerro Torre. Christ, it's not far; it hardly looks more than ten yards.

There is some elegance—and I find some solace—in the fact that I'm not good enough to stand on the absolute summit of this most perfect of peaks.

"Fuck it, I did what I did," I tell myself as I rappel away. "And I can always come back."

My body is tense, awaiting the first strong, swift blast of the west wind. I can feel the Lords of Patagonia marshaling their battalions. No two storms are ever alike; each one brings a new personality of spite. I dread the havoc of the storm so obviously on its way. The first rappels go easily, and back on the bivy ledge we retrieve our stashed gear. But then the wind comes on like a storm of spears. David and I work together atop the headwall. I catch his eye as I prepare to rappel past the edge. "Now we pay!" I yell over the wind. "Pain!" he shouts back, grinning. I continue to rappel first but can't dangle straight down the headwall. The building gale tosses me back and forth. At the end of the rope I reach for the anchor, but an invisible hand pushes me away. Finally, a lull. I lunge with the point of my ice axe, catch the anchor, and pull myself over.

To the west the sun is perched on a wall of clouds, and the wind rages like a mob of demons. Below the headwall I must go down and to the right, but the wind tangles the rope around lumps of rime. I yank on the rope as hard as I can to snap off the snags. Some won't break, so I swing over like a pendulum, tiptoeing on my crampons, and smash them with my axe.

We come to the small saddle that crosses over to the Helmet. Wind screams up the ice slope from below. I belay David, and he staggers across the saddle to disappear behind a rime monolith. The wind draws the rope between us into a taut 130-foot ballistic arc that doesn't touch the ground. The sun is gone, the sky is dark purple like a bruise, and we're fighting for our lives. Too scared to walk over the flat section of the Helmet, I crawl and feed rope through my rappel device until I reach the lip of the steep rime that drops down 200 feet to the platform below. I long to escape this scourge of wind, and I fumble with the ropes to rig the next rappel.

Two hours later we're descending by headlamp through the Col of Hope, that gigantic funnel for wind off the ice field, and it is a maelstrom. Golf-ball-size chunks of ice blast up the forty-five- to sixty-degree slope. The updrafts blow my clothes full of frigid air. Well after midnight we suffer down the final glacier in blackness broken only by our headlamps. Streaks of snow blur sideways through the pools of light. My face is stung by snow, and the gusts knock us to our knees. Then the slope runs out into flatness, and it's over.

At our gear stash below the Filo Rosso, we make a classic Patagonian mistake. Four people and eight hands pitching two tents, but somehow all eight hands are on one tent at the precise instant that a big gust launches the second tent into the night sky. The tent shoots through our headlamp beams like Dorothy's house going up the tornado in *The Wizard of Oz*. I hold the remaining tent while the others give chase, but we never see it again. Instead of a comfortable night spread two to a tent, all of us cram into the one remaining two-person tent and share some food and drink. David decides that he can't stand the crowding and builds himself a bivy sandwich out of the two sleds and sleeps between them. Everything aches, and none of us are comfortable, but everybody sleeps.

Stefan kicks us out of bed five hours later, just after it gets light. He has water heating on two stoves for breakfast. He wants to get back to Switzerland as fast as possible. An hour or so later we have camp dismantled and begin dragging our loads out of the Cirque of the Altars and away from the West Face of Cerro Torre. That evening, after six hours of hauling, we descend Paso Marconi into the Valley of the Río Eléctrico and spend the night.

Our time living in the landscape of our dreams comes to a close.

Ascent is past, the perils of descent have been negotiated. The laborious return to civilization is nearly done. The abyss no longer tugs at our heels. We are on flat ground. I see out to the steppes and can feel the future begin to take shape. I feel the steely, disquieting, fear-inducing wind. Some dreams have been captured, others yet pull us on.

·

The Cerro Torre campaign and the winter West Face, two ascents that beg comparison. Which climb was better? The answer is neither. The two sides of that mountain were different, each side is a wealth of experience, and I can't imagine my life without them both.

The West Face and the ice cap were the most outrageous landscape I've ever seen. Life on and above the ice cap was like an exile to an ice planet. Out there we might have been the only members of the human race. The winter West Face also has some ego-stroking aplomb: we scored a little bit of history (and one certain to draw some further footnote when someone climbs the West Face in winter and adds the final summit mushroom to the ascent). I am pleased to have played a little part in the rising evolution of that route and that mountain. What I did there with Jim, Alex, Stefan, and Charlie a few years before on the Compressor Route didn't even make a ripple—it had been climbed dozens of times.

But the first winter ascent didn't feel like a first ascent, in the same sense that the first ascent of a previously attempted route doesn't have the same feel as a pure first ascent, one where we are the first people ever to touch a particular slice of vertical geography. It was obvious that people had been up there before us, and for the most part we knew what to expect from the route.

Physically, though, the winter West Face was my hardest trip. I lost fifteen pounds out there—I lost only one pound at Ranger School.

Mentally it was my hardest expedition as well. I'm proud I didn't come unstuck, and there were times, particularly during that first attempt, when I was close. I built three fine friendships out there, and the four of us will be firm friends for the duration. We've since had great times in Santa Barbara and in Yosemite, and I look forward to climbing with them in Switzerland someday, but I wasn't at my best on that trip. I didn't have an edge, the edge of abandon that drives an ascent forward. There were gaps between my vision for myself, what I was actually capable of, and what I actually did. And an expedition is more rewarding the smaller those gaps are. My expedition goal is to be of one will, one mind, one action and to have no creeping calculation take me off the keen edge of the instant. I weighed my backpack, and loaded it carefully to make sure I wasn't carrying more than my buddies, and I loathe that moral weakness. The ideal me doesn't care; the ideal me takes as much as I can carry, takes whatever needs to be carried, and doesn't give a fuck what anyone else may or may not have. My ideal self does what needs to be done at every turn and doesn't need rest days, doesn't have bad days, and doesn't make bad decisions. My ideal self is always in good humor and makes everybody around me laugh. My ideal self doesn't keep score, and it makes things happen. My ideal self feels fear, just like my regular self, but it handles that fear well. And every time my real self comes up short of my ideal I hurt inside.

During my campaign on the Compressor Route I had no past and no future, and for two months I held the gap closed between my ideal self and my real self. I lived at my potential, in full accord with my vision. I had no failures of will, and I died no little deaths.

But then again, in those much more common times when you're *not* at your absolute best, you learn your exact capabilities.

•

In the morning we descend the last glacier and trudge around the rocky shores of half-frozen Lago Eléctrico. We stumble around the last bay and are faced with a 200-foot hill. It's nothing, it's really nothing, but I'm so physically drained that going up it almost breaks my heart. Later, we reach a forest and I walk in rapture under leafless trees. A dusting of snow covers the ground, but not enough to ski. We walk beneath the dark tortured shapes, well on our way back to the world of men.

THE BUS BOUNCES ALONG THE DIRT ROAD.
Every thirty seconds I run my sleeve along the fogged glass to
maintain my view. None of the other passengers seem interested in the brown blur of scrub vegetation that flashes past
the window. There is no conversation. The sameness of the
Patagonian steppe is terrible, faceless, and like an ocean. Many
souls aren't comfortable with their face to such a void, but I
think it's beautiful and I love it.

Later, somebody asks the driver to stop. I descend as well
and stand out in the desert. The wind is bitter and biting and it
shoves me away from the bus. I clutch at my hat and raise my
eyes. To the front left, across the road, the wind beats the waters of Lago Viedma to a white froth. Clouds churn over the
peaks on the far side of the lake, nothing but the bare outlines
of the closest mountains visible through the raging mists. The
toe of the great Viedma Glacier is just barely visible where it
calves into the lake. Down the road there is no sign of the
peaks I have come so far to climb. The future lies hidden in
those clouds. The cold penetrates with the wind, and I shiver.

The wind thumps my chest like a great hand, an invisible force that pushes me away from the mountains. Overhead, patches of royal southern blue show between dark racing clouds. No other vehicle is in sight on this lonely road. Grit blows off it and stings my face, and I step off the road to evade the flying dust. Green and brown buttes rear up to the right of the road. Geologic strata, contorted by an aeon, swirl like finger paintings through those hills. Clouds tear over their tops at impossible speed, but inside the wind plays through my heartstrings. Patagonia—it feels like home.

•

Seven weeks later, I sit in the entrance of a little shack walled with plastic in Piedra del Fraile, another of the base camps in this range. My body is sheltered, but rain falls on my elbow, which rests on top of a blue expedition barrel that stands outside the hut. The hard wooden bench numbs my butt and hurts my back. I stir and draw an idle pattern in the raindrops that bead up on the black plastic top of the barrel. A flurry of new drops ruins the pattern. I draw another. I look up and watch sheets of rain fly down-valley at an angle just under horizontal. The wind thundering down the valley seems to tap some universal fount of white noise. This alpine life boils down to great actions and great reposes, and I am a fool for those peaks and valleys. This is the twentieth consecutive morning of storm.

Kent McClannan, farther inside the hut, pumps pressure into a camp stove, screws open the stove's squeaky fuel valve, bleeds unleaded gasoline into the stove's pan, and sparks the gas into flame. This will be the fourth hot drink of the day. Trekker after trekker stumbles into camp soaked from soup to nuts. This storm has Kent and his partner, Bruce Miller, under building pressure. The rain puddles up in camp, and every passing hour of storm drives the blade of frustration further into their guts. They just hit the halfway mark of their six weeks in the mountains, and they still haven't touched Fitzroy. They have done nothing. *Nothing.* Except wait. Their frustration has tangible presence; it's like an elephant loose in camp. In the last hour, both have asked me, separately, what I think about the weather and whether they should change their strategy. Despite a decent track record of success in this range, one I know they'd like to taste, I have nothing constructive to say. All I know is that no storm lasts forever. I know nothing of the weather except for the painfully obvious fact that it is terrible right now. Today, like yesterday, and the eighteen days before that, we wait.

Jim Donini and I scored our two season-making first ascents in the weeks before Kent and Bruce arrived. We had more than enough good weather to do what we wanted. It doesn't seem fair. I feel absolutely no pressure to climb anything else this year; another climb would be icing on an already thick cake. I've been released from the wheel. Unlike in years past, it doesn't feel as if my whole fate hinges on the climbing I might do tomorrow. And besides, there is not one thing I can do about the weather. I wiggle my toes in fur-lined camp boots and nurse a cup of real coffee made in a French press. I put some classical music into my Discman and watch the clouds tear off the peaks, a wonderful blend of the modern and the timeless, like climbing itself, and my mind turns over the recent moments I spent sitting on top of Cerro Pollone's West Pillar, soaking up the best summit view I have ever seen in my life: neighboring Piergiorgio revealed to be a gargantuan fin of granite—we could see both its west and east faces. From our lookout above its head we could see down into the Torre Valley all the way out beyond Lago Viedma. The northwestern aspect of Fitzroy seemed at arm's length and there was the North Face of Aguja Poincenot, where we had had such an adventure three years before. Innominata's West Ridge and the West Face of Aguja Saint-Exupéry, the scene of two failures, lined up next to Poincenot, and across the valley from them rose the Southeast Ridge of Cerro Torre—the Compressor

Route—in profile like a cathedral's flying buttress. The Torre was in such good profile that we could make out features of the West Face above the headwall as well as the entire Compressor Route. I could see the little shelf where the Swiss boys and I had spent our last night on the Torre during the winter ascent, and Jim pointed out the spot where he, Stefan Hiermaier, and I had made our emergency bivouac during our stormy retreat from atop the compressor. We looked down into the horseshoe of the Marconi Glacier and down onto the virgin summit we had climbed a week before. And out to the west, running north and south in a thick band, lay the Southern Patagonian Ice Cap. There was hardly a detail in the range that we couldn't make out from that incredible perch. Patagonia, this beautiful and dangerous place, these mountains the very form of alpine perfection . . .

Kent's offer of a fresh dose of coffee pulls me down from my reveries. I badly want him to have a good experience in these mountains that I love so much. He richly deserves an opportunity to match his desire. In recent memory Kent has been bitten in the face by a dog, he was stung by a poisonous spider, he had half of the house he was renting burn down, his knee blew out, the engine of his car blew up, one of his best friends was killed by an avalanche, and he got stiffed out of a big guiding paycheck. He was working so hard in construction two years ago to earn a Patagonian season that he gave himself a hernia. Of course, he was working without any insurance so he had no choice but to spend all the money he had saved for the expedition on his hospital bills. That was a year ago. Incredibly, the same thing happened again just six weeks ago: Kent had another operation to repair another construction-induced hernia. This time he said to hell with it and came to Patagonia anyway. A lesser person would have abandoned his dream long ago. Kent has done nothing to deserve such a run of bad luck—he is helpful and generous, and he has been a loyal friend for more than five years. Both he and Bruce are far better climbers than I am by every measurable standard: better rock climbers, better ice climbers, better big-wall climbers. They're stronger and fitter. And that goes for just about every climber here in this range. That said, I've enjoyed one of the better recent runs of Patagonian success, and I don't know what I've done to deserve such riches. I don't sleep the sleep of the just. All I've done is climb when the sun shines and all I've done to deserve the sunshine is spend a lot of time in Patagonia.

But time alone does not account for Kent's Patagonian drought. He too has spent a lot of time in Patagonia; this is his second trip. Kent and Bruce are being denied opportunity. There is no way they could force a climb in this storm, and they know it. The weather is so bad that they couldn't even get themselves killed trying—against this wind no man could even hike up to the base of one of these mountains. There is nothing to do but wait.

What keeps Kent going against such adversity? Pride, determination, love, and desire. Desire to live his dreams, love of the alpine way, determination to play his hand through to the bitter end, and the pride a man takes in doing what he was made to do. We've both done the work. I've been lucky, Kent has not. His determination dwarfs mine. Kent is here pushing on, pushing on, right at the edge of what he can stand. Others around him let blisters and hurt ankles and upset stomachs deter their dreams. Kent tightens his belt to support his hernia, pulls a brace over his wobbly knee, shoulders his load, and goes up. The man endures, and I'd go with him anywhere in the world.

There were two climbers in town ten days ago showing off the promotional poster they made to celebrate the "important new route" they climbed here last year. There is no such thing, and this is a dumb place to look for glory. I'd much prefer the quiet respect of my peers. All mountain routes are meaningless unless, *unless,* they have meaning to us as individuals. There are no important routes, only good efforts, some capped with summits, some not. What alpinism is, is an incredible theater of character. During my season on the Compressor Route it was much harder to *not* climb Cerro Torre than it was to climb it. One effort was capped by spectacular success; one nearly cost me my life. But I'd rather be defined by that magnificent failure, the good fight. If I had not grown into a writer that experience would exist only between Jim Donini, Stefan Hiermaier, and me. It would be enough.

Climbing discussions usually fall into one of two camps: the one of conquests and triumphs, and the one of harmony with the natural world. The truth, like most truths, lies between. In the conquest and triumph stories, you almost expect a brass band to appear as the heroes approach the summit. I've never felt that kind of climax. Satisfaction grows as my fear and agony fade with time. And as for climbers always moving in a constant state of harmony with the alpine world, it may tell well, but it happens like that for me only in a few exceptional moments. My truth allows me moments when I soar, and a lot of trench warfare in-between.

I realize that my climbs and my climbing make little significant contribution to alpinism. They are not the hardest, the best, or the boldest. They are good climbs, I know enough to say that with full confidence, but they're not very important. What they are is tremendously important to me. They're the defining moments of my life, for it is in enduring Patagonia that I make my bones in my own eyes.

Jim and I have gotten good at this Patagonian alpine game, better than I would dare admit. Not better in the sense of being better climbers—I wager that we are among the worst here in that regard—but better in the intangibles. We arrive without a fixed objective, but nursing a few possibilities. Based on the conditions we encounter and on what we feel in our hearts once we're in Patagonia, we let our instincts reduce those possibilities to one clear goal. Once we identify an objective and agree on it, we do not abide distractions, vacillations, or second guesses. If we have to walk the whole distance from the trailhead to high camp with heavy loads in one awful day, then we do it, aches, pains, and exhaustion notwithstanding. We press on. We take no rest days, even in atrocious conditions, until our equipment is properly positioned for the climb. When it comes time to rest, we rest. We are efficient, even in the basic mucking about camp. We eat and drink a lot and we laugh. We know what stuff we need and we take it. If we forget something, which we usually do, we improvise. We try not to make excuses. We don't look back, only forward, and we go up. Our climbing technique isn't perfect, our system isn't perfect, our equipment isn't perfectly suited to the climb, but we go up.

I am a wealthy man. The depth and breadth of my Patagonian peregrinations are just that—wide and deep—and I can feel the campaigns of years past run through me like a free-flowing river. I have weighed myself in the balance of Patagonia and I have not been found wanting. I still want to go up there and prove it to myself like always, but whether or not we stand on top seems not as important as before. I have my victories, I know my defeats. It's enough to be up there, tooth and nail with the indifferent universe, at grips with my dream.

I don't come to the mountains because the world is any better up here. I come into the high mountains because I am so much better up here. Down in the normal world I seldom have life under control. The details escape me. I muddle in confusion. Solutions are not apparent. A lead bar of stress sits in my gut and motivation is a struggle to summon. That stress is more debilitating than the fear I find here in the mountains, the cold alpine fear that impels me to hot rages of action. Here in the mountains I ride the limits of my human potential. I feel no doubt about possible courses of action. I know what to do, how to do it, and I set about doing it. Here, I do not stomach compromise. I have become, like Jim, a goddamned, unrepentant alpinist, and our lives are victories, for we do not live like slaves.

J IM JUST CALLED FROM NEW YORK, WHERE he's doing slide shows. It's October, and I sit at my desk in California. In less than a month we'll meet in Patagonia for another round of alpine action. I'm surrounded by the weights of normal life: unpaid bills, unsorted slides, stacks of books, a dictionary, unfinished projects, the telephone, the fax machine, and my computer. What, exactly, is the mood of the night outside? I have no idea. Many good things happen in this room, but the war of attrition I fight here isn't clean alpine combat.

But four photos of Patagonia also sit on my desk and show clouds swirling around golden pillars of granite that rise from snowfields and are topped with ice. The pictures show the mountains up a valley that neither of us has, as yet, physically explored. What we will discover there, I cannot say, but the unknown, the unseen pull on me like gravity. To my now veteran eye these photos show a world of possibility. Patagonia reaches across many thousands of miles, and in my mind's eye I see the impossible blue sky and the walls of coarse stone that drop away below my feet. I look forward to being back in the alpine crucible with Jim. I can almost feel the first malignant caress of the west wind's return as it brushes my cheek, heavy and wet. I feel fear.

How remarkable, here at the start of the third millennium, to journey into a slice of geographic unknown. I thirst for the undiscovered country. Exactly where the coming voyage will take me, and what it will make me see, I can barely begin to guess. But one thing I do know for certain—I won't be the same man when I come back. Patagonia works its magic.

One essential question remains: Does alpine ascent have value? Is it a noble endeavor honored by the gods, or a sin against the will of God? *I do not know.*

To an ancient, the quest to climb an unknown mountain would have needed no justification. Nestor, the old charioteer, and the wisest of the Greek commanders who fought at Troy, would have seen in an instant that our endeavors were worthy of kings. To him, ascent would have held obvious value, for then life was not lived as an insurance policy. The quest was justification enough, and what a man brought back added value and quality to the whole world. The old gods gave no promise of paradise, and a man's deeds were his sole reward. The ancient world was alive with strange Patagonian sights, power and magic were everywhere, and mulish, mindless labor curried little honor among the gods. It seems to me a great thing to be able to say that in the mountains, my friends and I strive with the powers of gods.

But if the Christian God rules in heaven above, weighing the acts of man in scales of celestial justice, my conscious alpine choice defies His will, for we alpinists play fast and loose with the gift of life. What we bring back from the high mountains could well be like the water brought back to King David from the cistern of Bethlehem. The great king craved a drink of Bethlehem's water, but the Philistines held the city. Three of David's mighty men infiltrated the enemy's camp, stole a bucket of water from the well, and brought it back to their king. But David refused to drink, and he poured the bucket onto the ground. The water came at too great a risk.

In that case, I have made an intellectual choice for sin, for by climbing dangerous mountains, I do not honor the divine sanctity of life. I do violence against myself, against nature, and against God's will. If Dante is right, then, just past the bitter end, I will be condemned by snarling Minos to the Seventh Circle of Hell. There, sunk within the iron walls of Dis, my soul will morph into a black, twisted tree that bears no fruit and be tortured by the vile teeth of the Harpies until Judgment Day.

Perhaps ascent comes at the cost of my soul, but that would just serve to make it the more priceless. I cannot abide the thought of a gray righteous life lived among gray righteous souls. I will not live with only one horizon, spinning dull brown cloth and sowing a single plot of dirt. Do I choose wisely? *I do not know,* but I choose in full knowledge of the consequence of my sin. If that choice sends my soul into the eternal exile, then so be it. I will add my defiant voice to the cacophony of the damned.

In the meantime, I have my mountains.

LIKE THE PRACTITIONERS OF ANY TECH-nical endeavor, climbers have their own language, and like the language of any trade, the language of climbing has precise, spartan meaning. To butter this language over would be to turn the words in this story into tasteless mush. I have tried very hard to spin this tale of my view over the alpine parapet so that it rings true to the hardest of the hardcore at the same time that it tells it like it is to someone who will never climb a mountain. To do that I have used many of the words and phrases peculiar to climbing and climbers. Some are explained below:

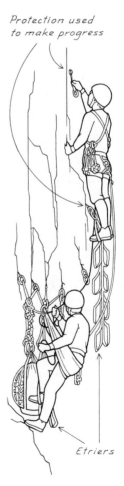

Protection used
to make progress

Etriers

AGUJA: In Spanish, "needle"; in mountaineering terms, a needlelike mountain.

AID CLIMBING, or **ARTIFICIAL CLIMBING:** When pieces of protection are placed in the rock and then physically pulled on to make up-ward progress.

ALPENGLOW: Low-angle sunrise or sunset light that colors the peaks pink, red, orange, or gold.

ALPINE STYLE: The style of climbing where climbers carry all their supplies with them and climb mountains in one push, without the support of pre-stocked camps and the security of a long line of fixed ropes. It's harder to succeed in alpine style, but it's much more of an adventure. Alpine-style ascents trade the risk of more dangerous descents for the benefit of being faster—climbers thus spend less time exposed to rock and ice falls, avalanches, and bad weather.

ALTIMETER: A device that measures elevation above sea level. It can also be used to chart the rise and fall of atmospheric pressure.

ANCHOR: Any point where ropes or climbers are secured to the mountain. Anchors can be made in rock, snow, or ice with hardware and slings. Anchors should be so solid that they cannot fail—if one does, it's usually fatal.

ASCENDER: A metal clamp used for climbing a fixed rope. A one-way cam allows these hand-held devices to be pushed up a rope, then to catch when pulled down. With an ascender in each hand, a climber pushes one device up the rope, transfers his weight to that ascender, pushes the other

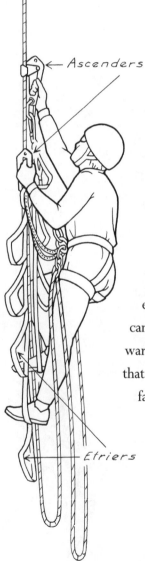

Fixed Rope

Ascenders

Etriers

ascender up behind the top one, transfers his weight again, repeats the process, and thus gradually works his way up.

AXE: An ice axe. An extremely versatile tool with a thin curved pick used for climbing hard snow and ice. Climbers usually carry two ice tools, one with an adze end for chopping ice and snow, and one with a hammer end for pounding pitons.

BAROMETER: A device that measures atmospheric pressure and is used to help predict weather trends. Also known as "the little box of lies."

BELAY:

1. The technique of managing a rope in order to safeguard a partner in the event of a fall.

2. An anchor. As: "I should be able to set up a belay just ahead."

BELAY PLATE: A device through which the rope is passed and then clipped to an anchor or harness with a cara-

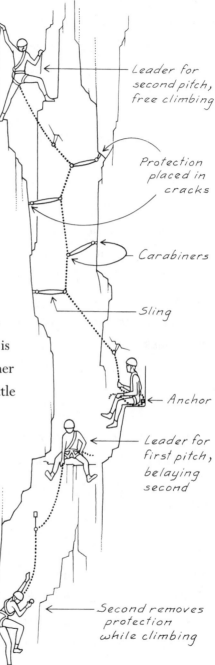

Leader for second pitch, free climbing

Protection placed in cracks

Carabiners

Sling

Anchor

Leader for first pitch, belaying second

Second removes protection while climbing

biner. This setup creates friction and lessens the force of a fall on the hands of the person belaying.

BERGSCHRUND: The giant crevasse found at the top of a glacier, where the moving ice of the glacier has pulled away from the stationary slope above. The upper lip of the 'schrund often overhangs the lower lip and creates a very difficult obstacle to ascent. Above the 'schrund and you are on the mountain, below the 'schrund and you are still on the approach.

BIVOUAC, or **BIVY:** A temporary camp where a team will spend the night.

BIVY SACK: A big uninsulated sack, like a potato sack, usually made of Gore-Tex. A sleeping bag can be stuffed inside to waterproof the sleeping bag, or the bivy sack can be used alone as an emergency shelter. Alpinists often carry just a bivy sack, planning to suffer a little in order to save the weight of a sleeping bag.

BOLT LADDER: A series of bolts placed within arm's reach, so that you can use the bolts to **aid climb**.

BOLTS: Permanent pieces of protection placed in holes drilled into the rock, either by hand with a hammer and bit, or by mechanical means. Bolts are the most time-consuming to place and the most environmentally damaging type of protection employed by climbers and, consequently, should be used only as a last resort.

BUTTRESS: A steep ridge. Picture the flying buttress of a Gothic cathedral.

CAMMING DEVICE: Technically "spring-loaded camming device" (SLCD). These pieces of protection have three or four cams on a bar that makes a T across the end of a rigid or flexible stem. A trigger retracts the cams, which can then be inserted in a parallel-sided crack. When the trigger is released, the cams open and hold the piece in the crack. The stem is then attached with a carabiner to a rope or sling. Any downward force on the stem translates to outward force on the cams, and that opening force holds the device in place. Some brand names for popular types of SLCDs are Aliens, Friends, and Camalots.

CARABINER, or **'BINER:** An aluminum snap link that serves a variety of climbing purposes, most commonly to connect pieces of protection to the rope or to connect the various parts of an anchor together. A locking carabiner is a carabiner whose gate can be screwed shut so that it cannot open.

CHIMNEY: A wide crack that a climber can fit entirely inside. Chimneys are climbed by putting pressure on the opposite walls and worming up.

COL: A high alpine pass.

COMMITMENT:

1. A climber's determination.

2. A term used to describe a situation from which it would be difficult or impossible to retreat down the same route used for ascent. (As: "Once we got above those loose blocks of rock we were committed, because there was no way we were going to chance it underneath them again.")

CONFLUENCIA: Spanish word for confluence. Refers to the junction of two rivers.

CORNER: A feature on a rock wall that looks like the corner of a room from the inside. Big corners are often called dihedrals or **open books**. In granite, there are often cracks in corners. Corners can be "right facing," "left facing," or "straight in," depending on their orientation.

COULOIR: A steep gash up a mountain face, usually with snow or ice in the deepest part. A steep gully.

CRAMPONS: Metal spikes that strap or snap to the bottom of boots for climbing ice and hard snow. The points that point forward from beneath the toes (the **front points**) are used to climb steep ice, and the points that project downward from the soles of the feet are used for flat footing on lower-angle snow and ice.

CREVASSE: A gaping hole in a glacier. Crevasses can be hidden beneath the surface snow. Because of the danger of falling through these snow bridges, climbers tie into a rope when they cross snow-covered glaciers.

CRUX: The hardest part, either of a particular pitch or of the entire climb.

DIHEDRAL: See **corner**.

ETRIER: Portable cloth ladders made of nylon sling material that usually have four or five steps and are used when **aid climbing**.

EXPEDITION STYLE: Climbing strategy that involves fixing lots of rope up a mountain and stocking a series of camps. This style was classically practiced during the Himalayan ascents of the 1950s. Maybe it was important then, but it isn't considered very interesting by modern climbers. **Alpine style** is where it's at these days.

FINGER CRACK: A crack the size of a person's fingers that allows a climber to jam in his knuckles or fingertips.

FIRST ASCENT: The first time a particular route is climbed. Kudos go to first ascensionists, who face the very real fear of the unknown during their climb.

FIST CRACK: A crack the width of a man's fist that allows a climber to jam a fist into the crack. Fist jams are generally not as secure as hand or finger jams.

FIXED ROPE: A rope fixed in place by being tied to an anchor.

1. Ropes left anchored in place to speed progress when the team returns in the future to make it easy (using **ascenders**) to regain a previous high point, or left in place below a climbing team to help them get down easily. Fixing more ropes than the minimum a team needs

compromises **alpine style** (which uses the same number of ropes as there are members of the climbing party).

2. When the lead rope is tied to an **anchor** so that the second can climb it using **ascenders**, it is said to be fixed.

FREE CLIMBING: Using just the natural holds of the rock to make upward progress and using the rope and hardware only as security. This is by far the most common type of climbing. Many laymen confuse free climbing with **soloing**.

FREE MOVE: One move upward, sideways, or even downward while **free climbing**.

FRONT POINTING: The technique used for climbing steep ice where just the front points of the crampons and the picks of a climber's two axes are punched into the ice.

FRONT POINTS: The one or two steel points of a crampon that project forward from under the toes of a climber's boots.

GAITERS: Removable nylon or Gore-Tex cuffs that cover pant bottoms and boot tops to stop the boots from filling with snow.

GLACIER: A great mass of ice that flows slowly downhill, like a frozen river.

GREAT SOUTHERN OCEAN: The great

Ice Tools

Hammer   Adze

Crampons

expanse of ocean in the Southern Hemisphere. Look at a globe from the bottom and you'll see that, other than the Antarctic continent, the Southern Hemisphere is almost entirely water. This ocean is the engine that creates and powers the awful weather of Patagonia.

HAMMER CORD: A length of string used to tie a **piton hammer** to a climber's harness so the hammer can't be dropped.

HAND CRACK: A crack from two to four inches wide where climbers can solidly jam their hands. Crack-climbing aficionados love this size of crack, because hand jams are very secure.

HARDWARE: Metal climbing equipment; usually refers to **protection** and **carabiners**.

HARNESS: Nylon webbing that climbers wear around their waists to attach themselves to a rope.

HEADLAMP: A battery-powered flashlight (similar to the ones miners use) that a climber wears on his head or helmet at night so that both hands are free.

HEADWALL: A large vertical section of rock or ice high on a mountain.

HOOK MOVE: An **aid-climbing** move made when a steel claw the size of a large fishhook is draped over a flake of rock.

ICE AXE: See **axe**.

ICE SCREW: A six- or eight-inch-long, one-and-a-quarter-inch-diameter threaded hollow tube that is screwed into the ice as a piece of **protection**. The holding power of an ice screw depends entirely on the quality of the ice into which it is placed.

JAM: A climbing technique where a body part is wedged securely into a crack and used for upward progress. (Jams can be finger, hand, fist, arm, shoulder, knee, or foot.)

LEADER: The climber who goes up first.

LEAD ROPE: The rope to which a leader clips the **protection** he places and the rope that is secured by his belayer.

MASSIF: A geographically compact but massive range of mountains.

MORAINE: The mass of rock debris deposited by a glacier: either a lateral moraine (on either side of the glacier) or a terminal moraine (deposited at the toe of a glacier) or a medial moraine created by the confluence of two glacial flows.

MUSHROOM: A term that describes some of the wild (and famous) formations of **rime ice** that festoon the walls and summits of the Patagonian Andes.

NÉVÉ: Snow that has been converted by a freeze-thaw cycle into plastic ice that is easy to climb.

OFFWIDTH: An awkward size of crack that is too big for fist **jams** and too small to admit a climber's entire body for **chimneying**. This size of crack is very scary and insecure to climb.

OPEN BOOK: See **corner**. Picture the pages of an open book.

OVERHANG: Where a cliff juts out like the eaves of a roof.

PATAGONIA: That part of South America shared by Chile and Argentina south of the Río Negro (about 40° south latitude).

PENDULUM: A technique used to cross a crackless section of stone by dangling at the end of the rope and swinging to the side to gain a new crack system.

PITCH: The length climbed between **anchors**, which is seldom less than fifty feet or more than two hundred.

PITON HAMMER: A hammer used to drive **pitons**. Alpinists typically just use the hammer end on one of their ice tools in order to save weight.

PITONS: Metal spikes that are driven into cracks with a hammer. Some of the names of the various types and sizes of pitons are knifeblades, angles, baby angles, bongs, birdbeaks, and lost arrows.

PROTECTION: Refers in general to the metal devices that climbers securely wedge in cracks and then connect to the rope with **carabiners** to shorten the length of any fall they might take. These devices are also used to build anchors. Nuts, stoppers, Tri-cams, camming devices, hexes, runners, pitons, and bolts are some of the many types of protection.

RAPPEL: The usual method of descending steep terrain, accomplished by sliding down rope anchored above. A doubled rope is employed (either from the midpoint of one rope or by tying two ropes together). The two parallel strands of rope are threaded through a belay plate and attached to the harness to create friction and slow the descent. Once the rappel is complete, one end of the doubled rope is pulled down from below. Rappels are dangerous because they are one of the few times that climbers are totally committed to their equipment, which most of the time serves only as backup.

RIDGE: A mountain feature where two upward-sloping faces come together.

RIME ICE: Ice condensed directly from the atmosphere, like the crunchy ice found in a freezer. In Patagonia the rime formations can grow into wild, twisted shapes; the biggest are the size of houses. They're almost impossible, and always terrifying, to climb—often rime can't support body weight.

ROCK SHOES: Tight shoes covered in rubber for climbing rock. Rock shoes can be slippers, low-tops, or high-tops.

ROOF: See **overhang**.

ROPE: Climbing ropes are made of nylon and are capable of supporting thousands of pounds of weight. They can be 8, 9, 10, or 11 millimeters in diameter and 50 to 60 meters long (165 to 200 feet).

SEAM: A tiny crack or weakness in the rock that is too small to admit fingertips.

SIEGE: A climbing strategy that involves fixing lots of rope up a mountain and stocking a series of camps. See **expedition style**.

SLING: A loop of tied or sewn nylon webbing that is used for a variety of climbing purposes, most commonly to connect the various parts of an anchor or to minimize the rope drag a climber going up first suffers when the rope goes around a corner or over an overhang.

SLOGGING: Hiking under a heavy load or through deep snow.

SNOW CAVE: A weatherproof shelter dug by a climber.

SOLOING: Climbing without a partner or climbing unroped.

SOUTHERN PATAGONIAN ICE CAP: One of the immense ice fields formed by the prodigious amount of snow that falls onto the Patagonian Andes. Said to be the world's largest nonpolar expanse of ice.

SQUEEZE CHIMNEY: A really tight chimney, just big enough to fit your entire body inside. They are usually awkward and unpleasant to climb.

STANCE: A spot on a cliff where a climber can stand relaxed.

TOPO: A sketch map of a route that has been previously ascended. Similar to a road map, it tells climbers where to go and what to expect.

UNION SUIT: A one-piece suit of long underwear. Union suits solve the problem of snow going down your butt and are warmer, but less versatile, than the equivalent two pieces.

VERGLASS: A very thin layer of clear ice coating rock that is very treacherous to climb.

WEATHER WINDOW: A period of good weather, long or short.

GREGORY CROUCH grew up in Goleta, California, where he now lives with his wife, DeAnne, and their son, Ryan. He has made more than a dozen climbing expeditions on four continents, most notably in Alaska and Patagonia, and his work has appeared in *National Geographic, Islands, Backpacker, Climbing,* and *Rock & Ice.*